Mark Time

The Book with Audio 4 CD Set

A different way to enjoy quality time
by reading and listening to Mark's Gospel
being read and explained

Gerard Chrispin

DayOne

First Printed 2011
Printed by Thomson Litho

ISBN 978-1846252846
Published by Day One Publications
Ryelands Road, Leominster, HR6 8NZ
tel—01568 613 740 fax—01568 611 43
email—sales@dayone.co.uk
web site—www.dayone.co.uk
North American—email—sales@dayonebookstore.com
North American—web site—www.dayonebookstore.com

Mark Time
The Book with
Audio 4 CD Set

**A different way to enjoy quality time
by reading and listening to Mark's Gospel
being read and explained**

Gerard Chrispin

This book is dedicated to all my friends who have encouraged me to share the good news of Jesus Christ with others, and especially my brothers and sisters in Christ and fellow workers in United Beach Missions, Missions Vacances, The Christian Answer, and Young Life. I so enjoyed learning most of the little I know from them. I should have learned more.

Contents
Mark Time—the Book with audio 4CD set

Foreword by Rico Tice

Associate Minister at All Souls Church, Langham Place, London
and author of *Christianity Explored*

Gerard Chrispin has spent decades working out how to teach the Bible with the utmost simplicity and relevance to young people on beach missions and latterly to men in prison. The result of all this experience is a commentary by a man, who again and again has stood up and said to himself, as he stands before his listeners, 'What is the one thing this passage has to say?' In section after section of this book you can see his preacher's heart isolating that one thought and causing it to walk off the pages of Mark's Gospel.

As a preacher who is focussed on Mark's Gospel, I have numerous commentaries on my shelf which take me through the detail of the book verse by verse and passage by passage, but I'm convinced from now on the first commentary I'll reach for is this one by Gerard because it will be so refreshing to see what the one thought from the passage is and how that has been communicated with passion and simplicity. It has often been said that to explain simply you must understand deeply and that, I think, is the hallmark of this commentary on Mark. I'm delighted to recommend it and hope that it will not only help the Christian preacher, but indeed will also be clear and simple enough for a person who is investigating the Christian faith for themselves and just wants a simple commentary on the shortest of Jesus' biographies. If that is you, as you read this preface, then may I assure you you've found a fine tool to accompany you on your journey into the Identity of Jesus (who he is), his Mission (why he came) and his Call (what it means to follow him).

Recommendation by Sir Jeremy Cooke

High Court Judge

Time spent thinking about what Mark says about Jesus is 'Mark Time', in the words of the title of this book. It is time well spent. Making the most of time means spending it with and for Jesus and living out the life He gives. Though we cannot have our past time over again, we can use 'time out' to get ourselves right for the future. This book (and the discussion course and correspondence course based on it) will help to do that. It comes with my strong recommendation.

A word from the author

The first Christian book I ever read helped me to establish my daily quiet time with God. It was John Blanchard's evergreen *Read, Mark Learn* (Evangelical Press). I am thus fully 'sold' on helping people to start their reading and study of God's word in Mark's Gospel.

I have enthusiastically promoted in prisons (and elsewhere) the *Christianity Explored (CE)* course, authored by Rico Tice. Using Mark's Gospel, without commenting on all of it, *CE* graphically and grippingly reveals the identity, mission and call of Jesus Christ, and seeks to apply it to those taking the course. *CE* is high on my course recommendation list.

It is, therefore, a great privilege to include a foreword in *Mark Time* from Rico Tice, surely one of Britain's most effective communicators of God's truth to day. I am grateful to him for his kindness. *Mark Time* follows a different approach from *CE* in our common aim to present Christ as the only Saviour of sinners. My burden is to see people reading through and enjoying *whole* books of the Bible. *Mark Time* thus seeks to explain the whole of Mark's Gospel, and to help understanding through its set questions.

I am also indebted to Sir Jeremy Cooke, who is not only a highly respected High Court Judge but a great encourager and a deeply committed Christian. For him to take time out of his busy life to read my book and recommend it is typical of his encouragement, and I thank him for that.

Mark Time—The Book with the Audio 4 CD set—is also central in the production of a separate Discussion Course for group discussion and an easy-to-follow Correspondence Course to promote personal study. Both the Discussion Course and the Correspondence Course use the *Mark Time* name and follow closely *Mark Time*—The Book with the Audio 4 CD set.

Finally, some more thanks! I am so grateful for his advice and careful initial internal editing of the text to my good friend David Harding, Pastor at Milnrow Evangelical Church and colleague in United Beach Missions and The Christian Answer (CA). Thank you also to my wife, Phillippa, who recorded Mark's Gospel for the CDs, and has given me many inputs on the book, the CDs and the two courses. Our gratitude goes to CA for putting the *Mark Time* written and audio prototype on their amazing website (*www.thechristiananswer.org/marktime.aspx*). Derek French (Grace Baptist Mission) could not have been more helpful. He both advised and worked with us on recording the CDs at GBM's studio. (At his advice, to give better recording 'flow', some wording on the CDs varies slightly from that of the book). He greatly encouraged and still encourages us by broadcasting the CDs to GBM's third-world audiences.

If you or those to whom you recommend *Mark Time* are helped by the Book, CDs, Discussion Course or Correspondence Course, I shall be a very happy man!

The publishers, Day One, and I would love to see *Mark Time* 'take off' in churches, fellowships and Christian groups and in many other places too. Prisons are obviously high on that agenda as Christian Prison Resources Ministries (CPR) seeks to make every aspect of *Mark Time* available behind bars, through the prison chaplaincies. We would also love to see it spreading out among military personnel, nurses, office and factory workers, students, home groups and many more. Some intend to use *Mark Time* to follow up people showing a real interest in the Christian message perhaps generated by a mission, a beach mission, a course, open-air meetings, other special meetings, regular Bible ministry in a church or fellowship group, or from personal discussions with Christians.

Some will just read the book. Some will listen to the CDs. Some will do both, either together or separately. Others will also join Discussion Course groups or undertake the Correspondence Course. Whether considering individuals, or large or small groups, our desire is to help many people to trust Christ, walk with Him daily 'in the light of His word', and know the joy of serving Him.

All this can only be by God's grace as the Holy Spirit uses 'the gospel of Jesus Christ, the Son of God.' (Mark 1:1).

Gerard Chrispin

Introduction

Welcome to *Mark Time*! We hope you greatly enjoy and get well acquainted with Mark's Gospel through this Book and through the audio 4CD set. This book and CDs are also helpful to use alongside any course on Mark's Gospel. Naturally that includes the *Mark Time* Discussion Course or the *Mark Time* Correspondence Course, both of which are tailored to and based on this Book and CDs.

To '*mark time*' can mean you set aside time to do something. '*Mark*' time also indicates that you are investing time in *Mark's* Gospel. Marching soldiers pause to '*mark time*' to await further directions before proceeding. Each meaning rightly applies to the *Mark Time* Book, CDs, Discussion Course, and Correspondence Course. Time set aside will help you, as you get to know this simplest and shortest Gospel and apply it to your own life.

The Gospels of Matthew, Mark, Luke and John, begin the New Testament's twenty-seven books which with the Old Testament's thirty nine books are included in the Bible's sixty six books. The Old Testament covers from God's creation of the universe until the coming to Planet Earth of the Lord Jesus Christ. 'Gospel' means 'good news'! Here is good news about the birth, life, work, teaching, miracles, death, resurrection and ascension of Jesus Christ. Learn how to come to know and follow Him, experience His forgiveness and help, and receive the new life He gives. That really is good news!

Each chapter of *Mark Time,* whether in the Book or CDs, contains the passage of Mark's Gospel covered in that chapter. *Mark Time* covers the whole of Mark's Gospel, from start to finish.

How can you best benefit from the *Mark Time* Book and CDs? (The Discussion Course and Correspondence Course each contain their own guidance about how best to use them).

1. Ask God to bless you by speaking to you through His word. Pray that He will help you understand and trust His word, and put it into practice in your life.

2. Read twice through the text of Mark's Gospel covered in each chapter of *Mark Time*.

3. Read and think through *Mark Time*'s explanation of the passage of Mark's Gospel. The book contains helpful sub-titles and footnotes not found in the CDs.

4. Play the relevant CD track twice and listen to the passage and explanation.

5. Consider the three set questions at the end of each chapter of *Mark Time*. The extra Bible verses noted will help you to be guided by other parts of the Bible as well as by Mark's Gospel.

6. Pray over what you have learned. Again, ask God to help you to apply that in detail to your own life.

7. Review it all later by reading and listening through the chapter of *Mark Time* again.

These seven points can be adapted where *Mark Time* is used for Bible studies, study groups, or for one-on-one teaching.

Mark Time may be used with any translation of Mark's Gospel. The four translations used in the book and CDs are:—chapters 1 to 4 - New International Version ('NIV'); chapters 5 to 8 - New American Standard Bible ('NASB'); chapters 9 to 12—English Standard Version ('ESV'); and chapters 13 to 16 New King James Version ('NKJV'). The Bible references function as follows: Mark 1:1-14 means Mark chapter 1, verses 1 to 14.

Enjoying Mark's gospel!

Mark's gospel read and explained in 52 chapters,

with three questions and supporting Bible verses per chapter.

Chapter 1
Preparing the way

Disc 1 – Track 02

> **Mark 1:1-13 (NIV)**
> ¹ The beginning of the gospel about Jesus Christ, the Son of God. ² It is written in Isaiah the prophet: "I will send my messenger ahead of you, who will prepare your way"— ³ "a voice of one calling in the desert, 'Prepare the way for the Lord, make straight paths for him.'" ⁴ And so John came, baptising in the desert region and preaching a baptism of repentance for the forgiveness of sins. ⁵ The whole Judean countryside and all the people of Jerusalem went out to him. Confessing their sins, they were baptised by him in the Jordan River. ⁶ John wore clothing made of camel's hair, with a leather belt around his waist, and he ate locusts and wild honey. ⁷ And this was his message: "After me will come one more powerful than I, the thongs of whose sandals I am not worthy to stoop down and untie. ⁸ I baptise you with water, but he will baptise you with the Holy Spirit."
> ⁹ At that time Jesus came from Nazareth in Galilee and was baptised by John in the Jordan. ¹⁰ As Jesus was coming up out of the water, he saw heaven being torn open and the Spirit descending on him like a dove. ¹¹ And a voice came from heaven: "You are my Son, whom I love; with you I am well pleased." ¹² At once the Spirit sent him out into the desert, ¹³ and he was in the desert for forty days, being tempted by Satan. He was with wild animals, and angels attended him.

Mark 1:1
The beginning

Verse 1 of Mark's Gospel says, *The beginning of the gospel about Jesus Christ, the Son of God.* An outdoor paint advert claims 'It does what it says on the tin.' The label on Mark's Gospel is: *the gospel about Jesus Christ.* 'Gospel' means 'good news' for the world about Jesus Christ. He is God's eternal Son coming to earth to bring that good news. Expect to hear much about Jesus and what He can do for you! Here is good news for today in a world full of bad news!

Mark 1:2–8
The baptist

But first, meet John the Baptist, God's messenger and prophet sent to prepare us for God's message of forgiveness through Jesus. His rough non-designer clothes match his simple, rugged life-style. He calls people to repent—a wholehearted about turn to God from wrongdoing. He immerses in Jordan's river those determined to live changed lives by repenting from sin. The Bible calls that 'baptism'. Humbly devoted to Christ, John stresses Jesus' worth and power. He feels unworthy even to untie Christ's sandals. John merely places people under water. Jesus places them under the life-changing influence of the Holy Spirit who will enter their lives. Though sinless, Jesus is baptised by John as His personal and public rejection of sin—the nearest to 'repentance' that this sinless Saviour can get. His baptism is also an example for us to follow. Additionally, it foreshadows the judgement for our sins which will totally engulf Jesus on the cross.[01] Jesus will then rise from death—like a baptised person rising from Jordan's water into fresh air.[02]

Mark 1:9–11
The blessing

The Bible teaches there is only one God,[03] eternally in three Persons: God the Father[04], God the Son[05], and God the Holy Spirit.[06] Each person of that Trinity now acts. Heaven opens when John baptises Jesus. Dovelike, God the Holy Spirit descends on Him. God the Father voices from Heaven His pleasure with His beloved Son. But Jesus will soon battle with Satan in real, personal and spiritual temptations.

---

01. 1 Peter 2:24.
02. Romans 6:3-4.
03. Mark 12:29, 1 Peter 1:2.
04. 1 John 4:14.
05. Hebrews 1:8.
06. 2 Corinthians 3:17.

Jesus alone is God's eternal Son. Yet each sinner trusting Him as Saviour becomes God's special child[07] in whom the Holy Spirit immediately begins His work, speaking through God's word, the Bible, as it is read, studied or explained. The Heavenly Father's help is always at hand in ongoing battles against temptation and Satan.

Mark 1:12-13
The battle

The Holy Spirit immediately leads Jesus into the desert for forty days of Satan's most subtle and powerful temptations. Often in His life Jesus is pressured to sin, or ease His pain, or prevent His death on the cross. Jesus never gave in.[08]

Temptation itself is not sin. Jesus never sinned, but He was tempted.[09] Temptation often follows or precedes personal blessing. If you trust Christ, expect difficulties. But God is in control and will limit your temptations.[10] He will help you.[11] Satan is real, but God will keep you.

Questions on Chapter 1
Mark 1:1-13 Preparing the way.

A. What does 'gospel' mean? Who is the gospel about? *John 3:16   1 Timothy 3:16*

B. Why is Jesus baptised? *Matthew 3:13-15   Romans 6:1-9*

C. What evidence do you see of the Trinity—God the Father, God the Son and God the Holy Spirit—at work? *Mark 1:9-11*

---

07.   John 1:12.
08.   Luke 4:1-15.
09.   Hebrews 4:15.
10.   1 Corinthians 10:13.
11.   Hebrews 4:16.

Chapter 2
The early priorities of Jesus

Mark 1:14-28 (NIV)
[14] After John was put in prison, Jesus went into Galilee, proclaiming the good news of God. [15] "The time has come," he said. "The kingdom of God is near. Repent and believe the good news!" [16] As Jesus walked beside the Sea of Galilee, he saw Simon and his brother Andrew casting a net into the lake, for they were fishermen. [17] "Come, follow me," Jesus said, "and I will make you fishers of men." [18] At once they left their nets and followed him. [19] When he had gone a little farther, he saw James son of Zebedee and his brother John in a boat, preparing their nets. [20] Without delay he called them, and they left their father Zebedee in the boat with the hired men and followed him. [21] They went to Capernaum, and when the Sabbath came, Jesus went into the synagogue and began to teach. [22] The people were amazed at his teaching, because he taught them as one who had authority, not as the teachers of the law.
[23] Just then a man in their synagogue who was possessed by an evil spirit cried out, [24] "What do you want with us, Jesus of Nazareth? Have you come to destroy us? I know who you are—the Holy One of God!" [25] "Be quiet!" said Jesus sternly. "Come out of him!" [26] The evil spirit shook the man violently and came out of him with a shriek. [27] The people were all so amazed that they asked each other, "What is this? A new teaching—and with authority! He even gives orders to evil spirits and they obey him." [28] News about him spread quickly over the whole region of Galilee.

Mark 1:14-15
What is God's good news?

Jesus proclaims *the good news of God*. Note four things. First, that news is for 'now'. He says *The time **has come***—meaning 'Act on this **now**!' Second, the ***kingdom* of**

*God **is near***. The King of kings has come. [12] Third, Jesus echoes John the Baptist's cry: *Repent!* Fourth, He urges everyone to *believe the good news*.

We too must recognise **now** our sin and the need of forgiveness by submitting to our Saviour/King. God's kingdom **has come**: King Jesus has come to Earth! It **will come** at His glorious second coming.[13] But His kingdom **does come now** when a sinner crowns Jesus as his King. The good news is Jesus died for our sins, bore our punishment, and rose again.[14] He forgives all who ***believe*** *the good news* by turning to Him as Saviour. 'I believe' means far more than 'I hope so', or 'I agree with that too', or 'I know'. In the Bible 'believe' means to commit to something. I really 'believe' in a chair when I sit on it, or in a medicine when I swallow it. To *believe the good news* means I commit myself to Jesus. I trust Him wholeheartedly, personally.[15] I become a disciple of Christ.

Mark 1:16-20
What is a disciple of Christ?

Christ expects all trusting Him to become real disciples. Here working men—fishermen—become disciples. Jesus already knows their names, brothers Simon and Andrew, and brothers James and John. He knows your name too!

He tells Simon and Andrew to come to and follow Him to 'fish' for people. He then calls James and John. Mark's Gospel often stresses that we must respond to Christ immediately.[16] All four follow and obey Jesus **immediately**. All leave their work. James and John also leave their father. Jesus now comes first. Each disciple of Christ trusts Him for forgiveness, follows and obeys Him, and 'fishes' for others to know Him. These disciples accompany Jesus to Capernaum on the Sabbath.

---

12. Matthew 21:5.
13. 1 Timothy 6:14-15.
14. 1 Corinthians 15:3-4.
15. John 3:16.
16. The Greek word *eutheos*, meaning immediately, is used at least 39 times in Mark's Gospel.

Mark 1:21-28
What is God's special day?

The Bible teaches that after creating the world, God rested on the 'Sabbath' day.[17] 'Sabbath', means 'rest' or 'ceasing'. Six days' work must be followed by that Sabbath rest.[18] Jesus' resurrection marks as special the first day of the week[19], sometimes called the Christian Sabbath, or Sunday, or the 'Lord's Day'. Jesus spends that first Sabbath with His new disciples in worship together (at the synagogue). Jesus teaches God's word to people *amazed at His teaching*. A spirit-possessed man is liberated when Jesus commands *Come out of him!* Christ's teaching and authority spread his fame through Galilee. Their first Sabbath involves the disciples in worship, witnessing Christ's power, and hearing God's word, the Bible. That is a good example to follow. The key is to spend time with Jesus. Everything else good flows from that!

Questions on Chapter 2
Mark 1:14-28 The early priorities of Jesus.

A. **What does 'believe' really mean? What does it not mean?** *James 2:19* *John 1:12   Romans 10:9-10*

B. **How do Simon, Andrew, James and John respond to Jesus? How can you respond to Him immediately?** *Romans 14:9   John 2:5*

C. **How does the way that Jesus' keeps the Sabbath give a helpful example to His disciples and to you?** *Isaiah 58:13-14*

---

17. Genesis 2:1-3.
18. Exodus 20:8-11.
19. John 20:1, John 20:19, Acts 20:7.

Chapter 3
Problems at home

> **Mark 1:29-31 (NIV)**
> 29 As soon as they left the synagogue, they went with James and John to the home of Simon and Andrew. 30 Simon's mother-in-law was in bed with a fever, and they told Jesus about her. 31 So he went to her, took her hand and helped her up. The fever left her and she began to wait on them.

Mark 1:29–30
Home and away

After leaving the synagogue, Jesus and two of his new disciples, James and John, go to the home of the other two, Simon and Andrew. Simon's mother-in-law lies in bed with a fever. After the early blessing of coming to Jesus, they immediately meet this serious problem at home. Problems at home may test us also soon after we have become real Christians. They can arise after God has blessed us, or spoken to us through His word in daily Bible reading or at church or chapel. It is challenging to live and witness for Christ. For some Christians, home is the hardest place to live.

Mark 1:30
How to respond to a problem

How do these four new Christians respond to this problem? Simply, they tell *Jesus about her.* That is what real prayer is—sharing a situation with the Lord openly and sincerely. These four men join together to tell Jesus in the first simple prayer meeting in Mark's gospel! It is good to pray together with others, as well as privately, about problems. I find it helpful in my daily prayers to pray 'sorry' prayers, then 'thank you' prayers, then 'please' prayers. First, I praise God for His cleansing mercy, immediate pardon, lovingly pure character, awesome greatness, majesty and power, and for His Fatherly kindness and faithfulness in hearing and answering my prayers.

Mark 1:31
What Jesus can do for a sin-sick person

Jesus heals Simon's mother-in-law of her fever by taking her hand and helping her up. She then begins to serve them! Note the personal concern of the Saviour and the help that He gives. God is always able to heal illnesses but often He chooses not to do so. In those cases He gives more grace and inner help to those who trust Him.[20] In the Bible we also often see our sin pictured in illness—which is not at all the same as saying that a given illness is a punishment for sin. That is just not true. But we are all smitten with the worst 'disease' of all, our sinfulness. It will cause our eternal death if not cured. Also sin, like fever, takes away our calm and peace.

Jesus took away the fever of Simon's wife's mother. He gave her the desire and strength to wait on them all, in loving service. So today, when we come as sinners to Christ for forgiveness, He heals us from our sin-sickness. He gives us His pardon, eternal life and sense of calm and peace. He is with us. Anyone whose heart Jesus has changed like that moves from the fever of sinful rebellion to the quiet calm of wanting to serve Him.

This woman was RAVAGED by sickness, RAISED by the Saviour, RESTORED to soundness, and READY to serve. Lives broken and spoiled by the dreaded disease of sin can also be completely changed by putting personal faith in Jesus Christ!

---

20. We see this principle also in the life of the apostle, Paul. Three times he asked for a troubling physical affliction to be lifted from him. God's response was, *My grace is sufficient for you, for my power is made perfect in weakness.* See 2 Corinthians 12:7-10.

Questions on Chapter 3
Mark 1:29-31 Problems at home.

A. As prayer is talking to the Lord, what does this passage teach you about prayer? *Matthew 18:20 1 Peter 5:7*

B. How can observing Simon's mother-in-law, before and after Jesus meets her, help you to understand how He changes people who come to know Him as their personal Saviour? *Matthew 11:28 John 14:27*

C. Although you cannot be saved by serving Jesus, should someone saved by Him serve Him? Give reasons. *Ephesians 2:8-9 Ephesians 2:10*

Chapter 4
The power of the Lord Jesus Christ

Disc Track
1 – 05

> **Mark 1:32-39 (NIV)**
> **³² That evening after sunset the people brought to Jesus all the sick and demon-possessed. ³³ The whole town gathered at the door, ³⁴ and Jesus healed many who had various diseases. He also drove out many demons, but he would not let the demons speak because they knew who he was. ³⁵ Very early in the morning, while it was still dark, Jesus got up, left the house and went off to a solitary place, where he prayed. ³⁶ Simon and his companions went to look for him, ³⁷ and when they found him, they exclaimed: "Everyone is looking for you!" ³⁸ Jesus replied, "Let us go somewhere else—to the nearby villages—so that I can preach there also. That is why I have come." ³⁹ So he travelled throughout Galilee, preaching in their synagogues and driving out demons.**

Mark 1:32–34
Power in healing

Sometimes people make extravagant claims about healing and some even profit financially and are self-promoting. Compare that with how Jesus heals. Here Jesus receives all the sick and demon-possessed people brought to Him. Jesus never heals, nor attempts to heal, every sick or demon-possessed person.[21] But He never fails when He decides to heal. The quiet authority of His word and presence suffice. His healings are not weird or stage-managed. Here, the whole city witnesses them. There is neither mention of Jesus laying hands on sick people, nor anyone being allegedly 'slain in the spirit'. It seems He heals a wide variety of illnesses and demon-possession—presumably including the hardest cases. As the *whole town* looks on, no failures or partial healings are recorded. Surely opposers as well as followers,

---

21. Estimates of the number of people Jesus healed usually vary between a few hundred and a few thousand.

observe Him? We learn that, because God can do anything consistent with His will,[22] He can heal anyone at any time, either directly or medically. He often chooses not to, but His healing attempts always succeed. Remember that His healings were before credible eye witnesses, including unsympathetic ones.

One day believers in Christ for forgiveness will be suffering-free and sin-free when they share Heaven with their Saviour who died for them and rose again![23]

Mark 1:35–36
Power in prayer

How interesting that Jesus, both fully God and fully man, chooses to pray. It is early in the morning and still dark. The place is *solitary*—Jesus prays alone. He acts simply and without gimmicks. He prays. Nothing else! If the eternal Son of God feels the need to pray like that, surely we also should invest quality time in personal prayer?[24] One mark of someone truly converted to Christ is that he, or she, really begins to pray. Some first pray what many call 'the sinner's prayer' from Luke's Gospel, *God, have mercy on me, a sinner.*[25]

If you love someone, you want to be with your loved one. If you have come to love Jesus Christ, whose love for you is incomparably great, you will spend time with Him in prayer each day.

Mark 1:37–39
Power in preaching

So Jesus prays before He preaches. We too should pray before serving God or doing things which test our strength or ability. Simon and co. find Jesus praying and tell Him *Everyone is looking for You!* Jesus replies that He will go to the nearby villages to *preach there also.* He prefers sharing God's truth to the empty praise of a curious, miracle-hungry crowd. Jesus has already demonstrated His ability to heal and cast out demons. Yet He says now that preaching God's word *is why I have come.* As He travels and preaches *throughout Galilee,* He continues to drive out demons.

---

22. Mark 10:27.
23. Revelation 21:4, Revelation 21:27.
24. Consider the Christian's former arch enemy, Saul. When he was converted to Christ some of the evidence given to prove his conversion to Christ was that *he is praying.* (Acts 9:11).
25. Luke 18:13

However, His priority is to make God's message clear. So how important it is for us too, to focus on His word, the Bible.[26] We should read it, hear it, trust it, learn it, live it[27]—and make its saving message clear to others. Christ's priority should be our priority too.

Questions on Chapter 4
Mark 1:32–39 The power of the Lord Jesus Christ.

A. What lessons can you learn from this passage about how Jesus healed people? *Luke 24:19   Luke 4:40-44*

B. Why does Jesus pray? Why should you pray? *John 17:1-26   Matthew 7:7 Philippians 4:6-7*

C. Why does Jesus regard preaching God's Word as so important? *Luke 8:11-15   Romans 10:17   2 Timothy 4:2*

---

26. 2 Timothy 2:15.
27. 2 Timothy 3:15-16.

Chapter 5
Leprosy!

Mark 1:40-45 (NIV)
[40] A man with leprosy came to him and begged him on his knees, "If you are willing, you can make me clean." [41] Filled with compassion, Jesus reached out his hand and touched the man. "I am willing," he said. "Be clean!" [42] Immediately the leprosy left him and he was cured. [43] Jesus sent him away at once with a strong warning: [44] "See that you don't tell this to anyone. But go, show yourself to the priest and offer the sacrifices that Moses commanded for your cleansing, as a testimony to them." [45] Instead he went out and began to talk freely, spreading the news. As a result, Jesus could no longer enter a town openly but stayed outside in lonely places. Yet the people still came to him from everywhere.

Mark 1:40-41
Love for the leper

A man suffering with leprosy was a complete outcast. He was separated from family, rejected by society, and barred from worshipping with other Jews. He was physically unacceptable and ceremonially unclean. He couldn't even visit the Temple. He had to shout 'Unclean' to avoid unintentional contact with others. Often leprosy pictures sin in the Bible. Sin does spiritually and eternally what leprosy did physically and socially. Sin's uncleanness defiles us, separates us from God, and excludes us from Heaven. People suffering with leprosy were excluded from civilisation: the Bible teaches unforgiven sinners are excluded from Heaven. Detailed Old Testament tests, run by the priests, determined if a leper was healed and cleansed.[28] Our Great High Priest is the Lord Jesus Christ.[29] Through His blood, shed on the cross, which

---

28. See Leviticus 14:1-20, for example.
29. Hebrews 4:14.

cleanses us from all sin,[30] we are freed from sin's leprosy when we turn our backs on our sins and put our trust in Christ alone.

How fitting that we see here Christ's great *compassion* for this poor man. He loves the unlovely, touches the untouchable, cleanses the impure, and cures the incurable! Jesus acts with this compassion over our leprosy of sin if we come to Him believing solely in His death on the cross in our place and in His resurrection life to save us.

Mark 1: 40-45
Lessons from the leper

We can learn so much from this sufferer of leprosy. Ignoring social and political incorrectness, he comes to Jesus! Neither his unclean state nor others' opinions prevent him. He recognises that only Jesus can and will meet his need. Still today Jesus alone can forgive sins, cleanse hearts, and be the way to God the Father![31] This leper is serious and earnest, not just religiously superficial. On his knees, he begs Jesus to cleanse him. *If you are willing, You can make me clean.* The response to his earnest plea from the Saviour will be the same for you, if you come to Him for cleansing from sin, mercy, pardon and restoration.

First, Jesus always forgives and cleanses anyone who comes to Him. Second, His cleansing and cure for sin is immediate. *Immediately the leprosy left him and he was cured.* Third, He demands that those asking for mercy should then obey Him as Lord. He warns the leper to obey the Old Testament law and show himself to the priest to verify, record and certify his cleansing. Knowing Christ as Saviour always involves obediently following Him as Lord.[32]

But this man forgets, ignores or disobeys Christ's command to tell no-one what has happened, but to go first to the priest. Instead, he tells everyone what Jesus has done for him. His enthusiasm is understandable, but this does not excuse his disobedience.

---

30. 1 John 1:7 (NKJV) – the NIV translates this *purifies us from all sin.*
31. John 14:6, Acts 4:12.
32. Romans 14:9.

Perhaps the examining priest himself needs to hear how Jesus can accept sinners? The leper's broadcasting of his healing restricts Jesus' freedom to move because of the seeking crowds. His work is frustrated. The ex-leper remains cured, however! God does not reject disobedient Christians, despite their disobedience!

We also need to catch the leper's enthusiastic love for Christ, and yet obediently follow the only One who can cleanse us from our sins.[33]

Questions on Chapter 5
Mark 1:40-45 Leprosy!

A. How do you imagine the man with leprosy feels about himself? Mark 1:40

B. How does Jesus regard him? Mark 1:41

C. As the disease of leprosy can picture how sin harms people spiritually, how can Jesus' delivering this man from leprosy picture how He delivers sinners who trust Him? Mark 1:42   1 John 1:8-9   Psalm 51:7-10

---

33.   John 14:15, John 15:10.

Chapter 6
When God is at work

Disc 1 – Track 07

Mark 2:1-12 (NIV)
[1] A few days later, when Jesus again entered Capernaum, the people heard that he had come home. [2] So many gathered that there was no room left, not even outside the door, and he preached the word to them. [3] Some men came, bringing to him a paralytic, carried by four of them. [4] Since they could not get him to Jesus because of the crowd, they made an opening in the roof above Jesus and, after digging through it, lowered the mat the paralysed man was lying on. [5] When Jesus saw their faith, he said to the paralytic, "Son, your sins are forgiven." [6] Now some teachers of the law were sitting there, thinking to themselves, [7] "Why does this fellow talk like that? He's blaspheming! Who can forgive sins but God alone?" [8] Immediately Jesus knew in his spirit that this was what they were thinking in their hearts, and he said to them, "Why are you thinking these things? [9] Which is easier: to say to the paralytic, 'Your sins are forgiven,' or to say, 'Get up, take your mat and walk'? [10] But that you may know that the Son of Man has authority on earth to forgive sins...." He said to the paralytic, [11] "I tell you, get up, take your mat and go home." [12] He got up, took his mat and walked out in full view of them all. This amazed everyone and they praised God, saying, "We have never seen anything like this!"

Mark 2:1–2
Jesus

Jesus preaches God's word to a large Capernaum crowd. God is at work! That produces surprise, blessing, praise, and some opposition.

Mark 2:3
The paralysed man

An unnamed paralysed man is brought to Jesus. We know nothing about him. He neither says nor does anything. He is a picture of our own inability and helplessness in our sins. We can neither say nor do anything to make ourselves acceptable to God. We cannot save ourselves. Only Jesus can do that.[34]

Mark 2:3-5
The four man team

Four men, also unnamed, carry the paralytic to Jesus. This illustrates prayer. A group can similarly bring an individual before Christ by praying together.[35] These four men first try to get their suffering friend to Jesus through the crowd. They cannot, so they use a less orthodox method! They make a hole in the roof above Jesus and lower the man down from there. They are so keen to see Jesus bless him that they think hard how to get their friend to Him. These men persevere until their needy friend comes face to face with Jesus. Christ sees and commends their faith. He meets the man's need and answers their faith by a staggering twofold miracle!

Mark 2:5
The miracle

Jesus surprises the people. He first forgives the paralytic's sin. His forgiveness is more important than his physical healing. Perhaps the paralysed man prays silently for forgiveness as He now realises who Jesus is? We don't know.

Jesus then tells him to take up the mat he lies on and to go home. The forgiven, healed man amazes the watching crowd by responding to Jesus' command. The people praise God for this miracle.

---

34. Ephesians 2:4-6.
35. Matthew 18:20.

Mark 2:6–12
The opposition

All this sparks opposition from religious law teachers, the scribes. Although they do not express their hostility, Jesus reads them like an open book. Throughout history, many religious people have strongly opposed Jesus. These scribes refuse to accept that Jesus is God and so object that only God can forgive sins,[36] thus disqualifying Jesus, in their eyes. They see Him as a blasphemer.

Jesus is in control: by His words and His actions He demonstrates His divine right and power to forgive sins. Christ's authority and God's work within the man immediately change the paralysed man.

Jesus can and will forgive us also, if we come to Him. But expect opposition from some who may not understand. Live graciously for Christ in front of them.

Questions on Chapter 6
Mark 2:1–12 When God is at work.

A. **What can you learn from the example of the four men who bring the paralysed man to Jesus?** Mark 2: 3-5

B. **Why is forgiveness even more important than being made well physically?** Romans 4:6-8 Psalm 86:5

C. **How does opposition to Jesus from religious people show that being religious is not the same as being a Christian?** Luke 18:9-14 Matthew 15:7-9 2 Corinthians 5:17

---

36. For the wrong reason, after drawing the wrong conclusion that Jesus is blaspheming, they rightly ask the rhetorical question, in verse 7, *Who can forgive sins but God alone?* Jesus is God, and He can and does forgive sins! That is God's prerogative.

Chapter 7
The making of Matthew

> **Mark 2:13-17 (NIV)**
> [13] Once again Jesus went out beside the lake. A large crowd came to him, and he began to teach them. [14] As he walked along, he saw Levi son of Alphaeus sitting at the tax collector's booth. "Follow me," Jesus told him, and Levi got up and followed him. [15] While Jesus was having dinner at Levi's house, many tax collectors and "sinners" were eating with him and his disciples, for there were many who followed him. [16] When the teachers of the law who were Pharisees saw him eating with the "sinners" and tax collectors, they asked his disciples: "Why does he eat with tax collectors and 'sinners'?" [17] On hearing this, Jesus said to them, "It is not the healthy who need a doctor, but the sick. I have not come to call the righteous, but sinners."

Mark 2:13-14
The master and the man

Jesus now teaches *a large crowd* by a lake. A despised and corrupt tax collector now yields to the Master's call. Jesus simply says to Levi, working in his booth, *Follow me*. Levi rises and follows Him. Both Levi's life and his name will change.[37] Crooked Levi will become disciple Matthew, and write Matthew's Gospel!

Tax-collectors were Jews willingly employed by the occupying power, Rome. They cheated ordinary people out of more money than was rightly due in taxes. Their own people hated them. Their Roman employers had no respect for them. Jesus knows all this as He calls Levi.

---

37. It is a miracle of God's grace and love that guilty sinners receive a new nature from God when they trust Christ and are *born again*. (John 3:3, John 3:7). God also gives them a new name—CHRISTians!

To understand Levi better, see how his name is spelled: **L – E – V – I**. He is **V – I – L – E** in the Israelites' eyes as a collaborator with the enemy. God knows all about his sinful extortion from ordinary people. He has an **E – V – I – L** heart of unbelief.[38] We share his basic problem, according to the Bible. Over his mind and understanding is a **V – E – I – L** caused by his sinful heart. That blinds him from understanding God's holiness and the righteous life God requires of him. If that veil is not removed, by trusting in Jesus to forgive him and give him a new God-conscious life, he will be lost eternally.[39] But there is very good news! Levi now begins to **L – I – V – E**. Resulting from his personal faith in Christ, he leaves his old sinful occupation and follows Jesus. This impacts many people. Someone is always affected when Christ changes a sinner's life! The wonderful truth is that his new life is *eternal life*.[40]

Although it starts as soon as you trust in Christ to save you, that life will continue in Heaven! That eternal life becomes yours by God's grace when you totally rely on Christ's death on the cross, punished for your sins there. Through His risen life, He will enter and indwell you as a forgiven sinner.

Mark 2:15-16
The meal and the misunderstanding

Jesus accompanies His disciples to eat at Levi's house with many other tax collectors and obvious *'sinners'*. Levi wants them to meet his Saviour. Again, Jesus meets religious opposition, now by the Pharisees. Like the scribes, they teach but don't keep God's law. Criticising Jesus, they show they misunderstand God's forgiving love by asking, *Why does He eat with tax collectors and 'sinners'?* They wrongly think they are superior to other sinners because they are religious. Jesus tells them *I have not come to call the righteous, but sinners.*

Like the Pharisees, do you think you are better than others? Do you refuse to turn from your sins to ask Jesus for forgiveness? Or do you see yourself as God does—a guilty sinner for whom Christ died?

---

38. Jeremiah 17:9 – I prefer the NKJV translation to the NIV: *The heart is deceitful above all things, and desperately wicked; who can know it?*
39. Matthew 7:13-14.
40. John 3:16.

Although, like me, you are a *vile* sinner with an *evil* heart, God will lift that *veil* for you, through repentance and personal faith in Jesus Christ.[41] Receiving eternal life produces a desire to *live* differently[42] and to help others come to know Jesus. But expect some opposition too as you follow Him as your Lord.[43]

Questions on Chapter 7
Mark 2:13–17 The making of Matthew.

A. What similarities and what differences do you see between yourself and Levi? Can the way that Jesus brings him into blessing be the way He blesses you too? *Romans 3:23 Jeremiah 17:9 Mark 2:17*

B. Why do you think that Levi was keen to get his friends to meet Jesus? How can that be an example for your own Christian life? *John 1:40-41 1 Corinthians 9:16-23 2 Kings 7:3-10*

C. Consider why people who are not Christians sometimes oppose those who are. Why do the Pharisees and Scribes oppose Jesus? *1 Peter 4: 1-5 Isaiah 53:5 Matthew 5:11-12 Matthew 16:11-12 Matthew 21:33-45*

---

41. 2 Corinthians 3:16.
42. 2 Corinthians 5:17.
43. 2 Timothy 3:12.

Chapter 8
What is fasting?

Disc **Track**
1 – 09

> **Mark 2:18-22 (NIV)**
> **18** Now John's disciples and the Pharisees were fasting. Some people came and asked Jesus, "How is it that John's disciples and the disciples of the Pharisees are fasting, but yours are not?" **19** Jesus answered, "How can the guests of the bridegroom fast while he is with them? They cannot, so long as they have him with them. **20** But the time will come when the bridegroom will be taken from them, and on that day they will fast. **21** "No-one sews a patch of unshrunk cloth on an old garment. If he does, the new piece will pull away from the old, making the tear worse. **22** And no-one pours new wine into old wineskins. If he does, the wine will burst the skins, and both the wine and the wineskins will be ruined. No, he pours new wine into new wineskins."

Mark 2:18
A puzzling question

Some people notice that Jesus' disciples are not fasting, unlike the disciples of John and the Pharisees. Puzzled, they ask Jesus why this is so. The Pharisees think they gain merit points by fasting,[44] though that is taught nowhere in the Bible. Fasting cannot make us better or worse before God and cannot make us accepted by Him. Only personal faith in Christ can do that. Neither is fasting a yardstick to measure others' devotion to compare it with our own. No-one should fast just to follow others.

Fasting is concentrating extra time in prayer in specific needy situations, or simply to get closer to God, by not eating for a limited period. In the spirit of true fasting, other legitimate privileges can also be temporarily suspended to concentrate on praying to God.[45]

---

44. Consider, for example, the Pharisee described by Jesus in Luke 18:12.
45. 1 Corinthians 7:5, for example, applies the principle to mutually agreed temporary suspension of intimacy between husband and wife.

Fasting helps us know God's help to say 'no' for a short time even to legitimate appetites, like eating, and enables us to experience His strength in doing that. Anyone fasting must do so secretly, in quiet sincerity, and not parade his fasting to others.[46] But God's people can also decide on fasting to focus on praying together for a great need. Each individual must decide if, when, and for how long to fast.

Fasting is often mentioned in the Old Testament. New Testament references include, seven in Matthew's Gospel (once referring to Jesus' fasting),[47] and five in Acts.[48] 2 Corinthians reveals that the apostle Paul fasted.[49] Only one day of Jewish fasting was stipulated by the Old Testament law, namely the Day of Atonement.[50] No-one has the right to command others to fast.

So how does Jesus answer the question asked about why His disciples are not fasting at this particular time?

Mark 2:19–22
Right fasting and wrong fasting

He answers by referring to wedding guests who are the bridegroom's friends. How absurd for them not to eat at the wedding feast! That would destroy the whole feast's purpose. (It would be different if the bridegroom had died.) Jesus is living with and amongst His disciples. That calls for joyfulness, not for fasting, at this time.

He also shows how silly it is to sow a new unshrunk piece of cloth onto older clothing needing repair. As the new cloth shrinks, it will make the tear worse. Similarly, to pour new wine into old leather wine skins will cause the new wine to burst the skins as it ferments. How ridiculous!

Something entirely new should not be attached to something old and perishing. They do not match, being incompatible. Jesus longs to give sinners eternal life and a new relationship with God involving receiving a new heart and a new spirit from Him.

---

46. Matthew 6:16-18.
47. In Matthew chapters 4,6,9 and 17.
48. In Acts chapters 10, 13, 14 and 27.
49. 2 Corinthians 6:5, 11:27.
50. Leviticus 18:12, Acts 27:9.

That relationship cannot come through continuing obsolete religious Old Testament habits. Jesus is at hand to bless those who know Him. That brings rejoicing! After His death there will be times for joint fasting and prayer—but that cannot be the main focus during His physical presence on Earth. To know Jesus brings joy!

Questions on Chapter 8
Mark 2:18–22 What is fasting?

A. Why is fasting helpful and right if it is correctly carried out? Why do you think fasting is unpopular with some Christians today? *Matthew 6:16-18   Luke 18:10-14*

B. What are some potential abuses or misuses of fasting? Why can fasting not save you from sin? *Luke 18:10-14   Matthew 6:16*

C. How do the two illustrations that Jesus gives (sowing a new patch onto old cloth, and putting new wine into old wine bottles) apply to fasting? *Matthew 6:1-8   Matthew 6:16-18*

Chapter 9
God's special day

Disc Track
1 — 10

Mark 2:23-3:6 (NIV)
23 One Sabbath Jesus was going through the cornfields, and as his disciples walked along, they began to pick some ears of corn. 24 The Pharisees said to him, "Look, why are they doing what is unlawful on the Sabbath?" 25 He answered, "Have you never read what David did when he and his companions were hungry and in need? 26 In the days of Abiathar the high priest, he entered the house of God and ate the consecrated bread, which is lawful only for priests to eat. And he also gave some to his companions." 27 Then he said to them, "The Sabbath was made for man, not man for the Sabbath. 28 So the Son of Man is Lord even of the Sabbath."

[Chapter 3]
1 Another time he went into the synagogue, and a man with a shrivelled hand was there. 2 Some of them were looking for a reason to accuse Jesus, so they watched him closely to see if he would heal him on the Sabbath. 3 Jesus said to the man with the shrivelled hand, "Stand up in front of everyone." 4 Then Jesus asked them, "Which is lawful on the Sabbath: to do good or to do evil, to save life or to kill?" But they remained silent. 5 He looked round at them in anger and, deeply distressed at their stubborn hearts, said to the man, "Stretch out your hand." He stretched it out, and his hand was completely restored. 6 Then the Pharisees went out and began to plot with the Herodians how they might kill Jesus

Mark 2:23-28
Sabbath opposition

God created the world in six days and rested the seventh.[51] That day is called the 'Sabbath', meaning 'cessation' or 'rest'. The importance of keeping apart one day in seven for God, as far as we can, is underlined in both Old and New Testaments. Read, for example in the Ten Commandments, in prophetical books, in Nehemiah, in the Gospels, in Acts, in Corinthians, and in the Bible's last book, Revelation.[52] No-one can be saved from sin by Sabbath-keeping, however. Legalistic insistence on how to keep the day, based on others' views or preferences, is wrong. The Bible gives clear principles and guidelines to follow and apply. God promises blessing to those who keep His special day holy.

The Pharisees oppose Jesus again. They claim His disciples break the Sabbath by picking and eating heads of grain as they walk through the fields with Jesus. Clearly Jesus had not stopped them eating the grain! The Pharisees observe many superficial rules about what is permitted on the Sabbath. Their rules are not in the Old Testament. The Pharisees furiously oppose Christ's disciples' liberty to keep the Sabbath sensibly and biblically.

Jesus answers them by underlining the real spirit of Sabbath-keeping. He indicates legitimate God-allowed exceptions to the 'no work' principle.[53] They still apply today in keeping Sunday, the Lord's Day, as the Christian Sabbath, which also celebrates Christ's resurrection from the dead.

First, Jesus shows that King David's ravenous followers ate the priests' consecrated bread in the Temple.[54] Survival was more important than religious form and ceremony. It is right to prepare and eat food on the Sabbath. Jesus says that *The Sabbath was made for man, not man for the Sabbath* and that *the Son of Man is Lord even of the Sabbath.* He wants the Sabbath to be kept properly and sensibly.

---

51. Genesis 2:1-3.
52. Exodus 20:8-11, Deuteronomy 5:12-15, Isaiah 56:1-8, Isaiah 58:13-14, Jeremiah 17:19-27, Ezekiel 20:10-32, Nehemiah 13:15-22, Nehemiah 10:28- 31, Mark 2:23-8, Matthew 24:14-23, Acts 4:10-12 (cf Psalm 118:22-24, Ephesians 2:20, 1 Peter 2:4-8), Acts 20:7, 1 Corinthians 16:1-2, Revelation 1:10.
53. For example in Matthew 12:1-22.
54. 1 Samuel 21:1-6.

Mark 3:1-6
Doing good on the Sabbath

Criticised for speaking to a man about healing his withered hand on the Sabbath in the synagogue, Jesus simply asks if it is right to do good or to do evil. Should He save life or kill on the Sabbath? They remain silent. Distressed and angry at their hypocrisy, Jesus heals the man's hand. His example shows it is always right to serve sick and needy people on the Sabbath. That is an excellent use of the Sabbath, or Jesus would not have healed the man then.

Again this produces cruel and unjustified opposition from the hypocritical Pharisees. They plot together with their traditional enemies, the Herodians, a secular political party supporting Rome, to kill Jesus. Opposition to Jesus and His gospel is never logical. It comes from sinful rebel hearts.

As Jesus heals, His opponents scheme to kill the only completely innocent Man! If Jesus' healing of the man is supposed to be wrong on the Sabbath, how much worse is their murderous intent? It is easy to criticise those whose lives put ours to shame.

Questions on Chapter 9
Mark 2:23-3:6 God's special day.

A. **What disciplines, blessings and advantages can Christians expect in keeping the Lord's Day, Sunday, as the Christian Sabbath? Why do you think that relatively few Christians seem to take it seriously today?** Mark 2:27-28 Exodus 20:8-11 Isaiah 58:13-14 Matthew 7:6-9

B. **In this passage, what does Jesus do on the Sabbath, and why?** Mark 3:1-6

C. **Can you gain forgiveness by keeping the Sabbath? Can you lose eternal life by not keeping the Sabbath? If salvation does not depend upon keeping the Sabbath, why is it so important to keep it?** Galatians 2:16 John 3:15-16 Romans 6:23 1 John 5:11-13

Chapter 10
Different attitudes towards Jesus

Mark 3:7-21 (NIV)
⁷ Jesus withdrew with his disciples to the lake, and a large crowd from Galilee followed. ⁸ When they heard all he was doing, many people came to him from Judea, Jerusalem, Idumea, and the regions across the Jordan and around Tyre and Sidon. ⁹ Because of the crowd he told his disciples to have a small boat ready for him, to keep the people from crowding him. ¹⁰ For he had healed many, so that those with diseases were pushing forward to touch him. ¹¹ Whenever the evil spirits saw him, they fell down before him and cried out, "You are the Son of God." ¹² But he gave them strict orders not to tell who he was.

¹³ Jesus went up on a mountainside and called to him those he wanted, and they came to him. ¹⁴ He appointed twelve— designating them apostles— that they might be with him and that he might send them out to preach ¹⁵ and to have authority to drive out demons. ¹⁶ These are the twelve he appointed: Simon (to whom he gave the name Peter); ¹⁷ James son of Zebedee and his brother John (to them he gave the name Boanerges, which means Sons of Thunder); ¹⁸ Andrew, Philip, Bartholomew, Matthew, Thomas, James son of Alphaeus, Thaddaeus, Simon the Zealot ¹⁹ and Judas Iscariot, who betrayed him. ²⁰ Then Jesus entered a house, and again a crowd gathered, so that he and his disciples were not even able to eat. ²¹ When his family heard about this, they went to take charge of him, for they said, "He is out of his mind."

Mark 3:7–21
The disciples' devotion

Jesus withdraws with His disciples to the lake. After meeting the gathered crowd, His disciples arrange for a boat to give Jesus space to preach. Later Jesus ascends a mountain to call and choose twelve disciples. Their priorities are, first, to spend time with Him and, second, to go to preach and drive out demons with Jesus' unique authority. The twelve are Simon Peter, James, John, Andrew, Philip, Bartholomew, Matthew, Thomas, James, Thaddeus, Simon the Zealot, and Judas Iscariot, His eventual betrayer.

Learn from this historic and unrepeatable event that it is important to serve Jesus in preaching His word and helping with people and in practical matters. Christians should serve like this in the fellowship of a church where people love Christ, His word and His gospel.

But the first priority must always be to spend time with Jesus Christ Himself, in personal devotion to Him. We should spend daily quality time alone with Him reading, studying His word, and praying. Our prayers should include confession, praise, thanksgiving, making requests, and praying for others. Devotion to Christ is the springboard for serving Him.

Mark 3:7-12
The crowd's curiosity

Between leaving the lake and climbing the mountain, Jesus and the disciples are with the crowd. Many people come from Galilee and around. Jesus heals diseased people pushing forward to touch Him, and He deals with spirit-possessed victims. They recognise Him as the Son of God. Jesus orders them not to tell others about Him. That is His disciples' task as they trust, obey, and serve Him. The crowd's attitudes towards Jesus will vary from curiosity to conviction, and from being comforted to being challenged. So many crowd around that Jesus and His disciples cannot eat a well deserved meal. Curious crowds follow crazes or popular fads, but only His trusting and following disciples will take time to get to know Him well.

Mark 3:21
The family's failure

Jesus' mother and immediate family fail to recognise who He is and what He does, despite His well attested miracles and obvious unique authority. Family members come to take Him, saying He is insane!

Someone rightly said that Jesus must be either bad, or mad or God. The Bible documents His purity and righteousness [55]—He certainly is not 'bad'. His sanity is such that no-one could contradict Him logically.[56] He is not 'mad'. That leaves only one option—proven, proclaimed and made clear in The Bible. Jesus is God.[57] 'Jesus' means 'God saves'. He is the eternal God in flesh who alone can save us from death and Hell. Our attitude to Him should be one of total trust and submission.

Questions on Chapter 10
Mark 3:7–21 Different attitudes towards Jesus.

A. Why should the disciples of Jesus spend time with Him before going out to serve Him? *Mark 3:14 Luke 10:38-42 John 15:5 Psalm 91:1*

B. Do you think the crowd was really seeking God or just being curious about Christ's miracles? Does verse 12 give you a clue? *Mark 3:8 Jeremiah 29:13 Mark 7:6*

C. How and why do Jesus' family misjudge Him so badly? Should any family opposition prevent us from following Him? *Mark 3:21 John 1:11 Mark 6:4*

---

55. Romans 5:18, 1 John 2:1, John 2:29.
56. John 7:45-46.
57. John 8:58, John 14:8-9.

Chapter 11
What is the unpardonable sin?

Disc 1 – Track 12

> **Mark 3:22-30 (NIV)**
> **22** And the teachers of the law who came down from Jerusalem said, "He is possessed by Beelzebub! By the prince of demons he is driving out demons." **23** So Jesus called them and spoke to them in parables: "How can Satan drive out Satan? **24** If a kingdom is divided against itself, that kingdom cannot stand. **25** If a house is divided against itself, that house cannot stand. **26** And if Satan opposes himself and is divided, he cannot stand; his end has come. **27** In fact, no-one can enter a strong man's house and carry off his possessions unless he first ties up the strong man. Then he can rob his house. **28** I tell you the truth, all the sins and blasphemies of men will be forgiven them. **29** But whoever blasphemes against the Holy Spirit will never be forgiven; he is guilty of an eternal sin." **30** He said this because they were saying, "He has an evil spirit."

Mark 3:22
The blasphemous accusation

The teachers of the law from Jerusalem now build on the accusation of Jesus' family that *He is out of His mind.* Worse, they say that Jesus is actually possessed by Beelzebub, the prince of demons when He casts out demons by Beelzebub. That terrible allegation is particularly grave and disastrous to make against the holy Son of God.

Mark 3:23-27
The logical answer of Jesus

Jesus responds with telling logic. *How can Satan cast out Satan?*, He asks. Would

Satan oppose himself? Would he destroy his own kingdom? His evil household would be torn apart and could not stand.

A robber of an occupied house must overcome the occupier. If the occupier is strong, that is harder. He must be bound first. Why would Satan tie himself up? That's nonsense.

Mark 3:28-30
Jesus teaches about the unpardonable sin

The 'unpardonable sin' worries some Christians unnecessarily. The teaching of Matthew's [58] and Luke's [59] Gospels shows the unpardonable sin is the malicious, blasphemous, intentional, continuing attributing to Satan the works done by the Holy Spirit through Christ and in Christ's people. The Holy Spirit's work is regarded as evil and Satanic. No one believing that can have forgiveness. That sin cannot be committed accidentally. It is unforgivable because it progressively hardens the heart. The offender finally cannot sense God's Holy Spirit convicting him. His conscience becomes so calloused and hardened that he never senses his need to repent and ask for forgiveness. He *will suddenly be destroyed—beyond remedy.*[60]

Anyone committing *that* sin never has been forgiven and never can be. *He is guilty of an eternal sin.* It is impossible for someone who has turned from sin to Jesus Christ to ever commit it.[61] Someone who is so conscience-stricken and anxious about having committed the unpardonable sin that he asks for forgiveness for it demonstrates thereby that the Holy Spirit is working in his life. That's why he is convicted of sin. Clearly he is not abandoned by the Holy Spirit, who is convicting him to bring him to repentance.

Committing the unpardonable sin makes the offender so hard hearted that he cannot feel his need of forgiveness. If you feel so guilty that you determine not to repeat the sin again, you cannot have committed it! Your attitude shows *real* repentance—not just remorse, which is merely feeling sorry for yourself. Judas showed remorse and

---

58. Matthew 12:22-37.
59. Luke 11:14-26.
60. Proverbs 29:1.
61. John 10:27-30.

regret, but not repentance leading him to be forgiven and saved.[62]

To all who have repented and received Christ as their Saviour and Lord, God's message is that *the blood of Jesus Christ, His Son, cleanses from all sin*.[63] Rejoice in God's complete and eternal acceptance if you know Jesus as your Saviour. If not, you need to trust Him now. The Bible says *Everyone who calls on the name of the LORD shall be saved*.[64]

Questions on Chapter 11
Mark 3:22–30 What is the unpardonable sin?

A. **Based on *this* passage what do you notice about the 'unpardonable sin'? How does it help also to look at other passages from the Gospels and blend them together?** Mark 3:22, 30   Matthew 12:22-37   Luke 11:14-16

B. **Is the unpardonable sin just a case of bad backsliding?** Mark 3:29   1 John 1:7   Romans 5:10

C. **How could 1 John 1:7 and Romans 10:13 help you to comfort a Christian who is really worried about having committed the unpardonable sin?** 1 John 1:7   Romans 10:13

---

62. Matthew 27:3.
63. 1 John 1:7 (NKJV).
64. Romans 10:13.

Chapter 12
Two families

Disc 1 — Track 13

> **Mark 3:31-35 (NIV)**
> ³¹ **Then Jesus' mother and brothers arrived. Standing outside, they sent someone in to call him.** ³² **A crowd was sitting around him, and they told him, "Your mother and brothers are outside looking for you."** ³³ **"Who are my mother and my brothers?" he asked.** ³⁴ **Then he looked at those seated in a circle around him and said, "Here are my mother and my brothers!** ³⁵ **Whoever does God's will is my brother and sister and mother."**

Mark 3:31-32
Our natural family

We met Jesus' natural family in verse 21. Now they arrive *to take charge of Him* because they wrongly think *He is out of His mind.* His mother and brothers send someone to find Him. Even His godly mother, Mary, now misunderstands her divinely conceived Son.

Like Jesus, we all are born into natural families, however scattered and divided our families may be. Unlike Him, we all have two biological parents. Many also have brothers, sisters, grandparents, aunts, uncles, nephews and nieces; whether as full blood relatives, half-blood relatives, or adopted members of our family. From prison to palace, families vary greatly. Some never know their parents or are badly let down, misunderstood, or even abused by them. Others have loyal, caring, providing parents whose love includes much needed balanced discipline. Some are abandoned or ignored by family members. Others, who are supported and encouraged, have great confidence that their families appreciate and know them well.

Whatever our family experience, God expects from us the highest moral conduct, faithfulness and, when possible, loving care and support for family members. This includes husbands and wives, parents and children, and brothers and sisters.[65] For example, I should 'honour' my parents[66] even if their wrong conduct means I have lost affection and respect for them. That is difficult, but God is at hand to help. The first family member to trust Jesus often influences others who also turn from their sins and come to Him for forgiveness and a wonderful new start.

Mark 3:33-35
Our new family

Jesus, surrounded by a crowd, hears that His mother and brothers have come for Him. He makes people think when He says *Who are my mother and brothers?* Looking at those nearest to Him—His disciples—He declares that they are His closest family! He then explains that *Whoever does God's will is my brother and sister and mother.*

When Jesus later expresses His loving care for Mary, as He hangs nailed to the cross, we see how close He is to her.[67] But now He speaks of an even closer spiritual and eternal family which, however, does not replace His natural family. Every Christian belongs also to that family. It is wonderful when members of our natural family trust Jesus and become members of our new family in Christ! That is the best of both worlds! To become a member of God's new family, with God the Father as our father, God the Son as our Saviour, and God the Spirit as our constant comforter, John 1:12 says that we must receive Christ into our hearts. That part of doing God's will makes us His blood-bought children, through the sacrifice of Jesus for us. We continue doing His will by living to please God, as He helps and strengthens us. Are you in this new family yet?

---

65. Colossians 3:18-21.
66. Exodus 20:12.
67. John 19:26.

Questions on Chapter 12
Mark 3:31–35 Two families.

A. **What privileges are there in belonging to a close and helpful family whose members love and help each other?** *Matthew 7: 9-10*

B. **What are the even greater privileges of belonging to God's family by receiving Jesus Christ as Saviour and becoming a 'born again' child of God?**
John 1:12   Matthew 7: 11   Matthew 6:9-15   John 3:3-8

C. **How should a Christian relate both to his or her natural family and to his or her new Christian family?** *Exodus 20:12   1 John 2:12-14   1 Timothy 5:1-3*

Chapter 13
The parable of the four soils

Mark 4:1-20 (NIV)
[1] Again Jesus began to teach by the lake. The crowd that gathered round him was so large that he got into a boat and sat in it out on the lake, while all the people were along the shore at the water's edge. [2] He taught them many things by parables, and in his teaching said: [3] "Listen! A farmer went out to sow his seed. [4] As he was scattering the seed, some fell along the path, and the birds came and ate it up. [5] Some fell on rocky places, where it did not have much soil. It sprang up quickly, because the soil was shallow. [6] But when the sun came up, the plants were scorched, and they withered because they had no root. [7] Other seed fell among thorns, which grew up and choked the plants, so that they did not bear grain. [8] Still other seed fell on good soil. It came up, grew and produced a crop, multiplying thirty, sixty, or even a hundred times." [9] Then Jesus said, "He who has ears to hear, let him hear." [10] When he was alone, the Twelve and the others around him asked him about the parables. [11] He told them, "The secret of the kingdom of God has been given to you. But to those on the outside everything is said in parables [12] so that, "'they may be ever seeing but never perceiving, and ever hearing but never understanding; otherwise they might turn and be forgiven!'" [13] Then Jesus said to them, "Don't you understand this parable? How then will you understand any parable? [14] The farmer sows the word. [15] Some people are like seed along the path, where the word is sown. As soon as they hear it, Satan comes and takes away the word that was sown in them. [16] Others, like seed sown on rocky places, hear the word and at once receive it with joy. [17] But since they have no root, they last only a short time. When trouble or persecution comes because of the word, they quickly fall away. [18] Still others, like seed sown among thorns, hear the word; [19] but the worries of this life, the deceitfulness of wealth and the desires for other things come in and choke the word, making

it unfruitful. 20 Others, like seed sown on good soil, hear the word, accept it, and produce a crop—thirty, sixty or even a hundred times what was sown."

Mark 4:1–3

The sermon at the shore

Crowds come to hear Jesus preach from a boat on the lake. He teaches *many things by parables*. A parable is an earthly story with a heavenly meaning. Jesus uses everyday things to illustrate the things of God. Here he talks about different soils and a farmer sowing seed to grow crops.

Mark 4:4–12

The seed and the soils

Similar seed is sown on each type of soil. There are four kinds of soil into which the seed falls. Some soil forms the pathway, doubtless made harder as the farmer treads on it while sowing the seed. The birds quickly eat that seed. Secondly, there is shallow soil in rocky ground, where immediate growth from the seed sown withers as the sun beats down on it. It has no roots. Thirdly, the seed sown amongst thorns produces short-lived growth. Then thorns choke the crop and no grain is produced. Finally, good soil yields good crops in varying amounts.

Jesus tells his listeners to pay attention. His disciples then ask what He means. Jesus replies that only His disciples can understand God's word. His parables are like coded secrets. Only someone knowing and following Him as His disciple will grasp what Jesus teaches. Encouragingly, the simplest sinner trusting Christ as personal Saviour, begins to understand God's word as God's Holy Spirit enlightens His mind. [68]

---

68. Ephesians 1:18.

Mark 4:13-20
The sorts of soil

Jesus explains to His disciples that each soil receiving the seed of God's word stands for a different group of hearers. The pathway's hardened soil represents those who hear God's message but instantly lose it as Satan snatches away the seed, like the hungry birds. We must consider seriously what we read in, or hear explained from, the Bible. The soil amongst the rocks, producing quick growth before the sun withers the crop, is like people initially receiving God's truth joyfully. But, being shallow, when tested by troubles or opposition by persecution, they wither. This reminds us to 'pray in' what God tells us through His word and to trust Him in hardships. The third soil, where thorns choke the crop, stands for hearers becoming unfruitful because they get choked by life's worries, wealth's deceitful pull, or materialistic desires to own things. We must set our minds on eternity.[69] Heaven will be ours if we turn earnestly to Christ and His word,[70] but Hell awaits those who put other things before knowing Christ's pardon and Lordship, and following Him in the light of the Bible's teaching.[71]

But be encouraged! There is good soil too! Its yield varies. It reminds us that anyone who humbly hears or reads God's word, trusts it, submits to its teaching, and puts it into practice with God's help, will be saved eternally and bring forth the fruit of a new life in Christ now. That good soil, therefore, represents those who are saved by Jesus Christ. It is clear from His teaching that no one will understand any other parable unless he or she understands this one. Which sort of soil are you?

Questions on Chapter 13
Mark 4:1-20 The parable of the four soils.

A. How would you describe a parable? Why does Jesus use parables?
Matthew 13:34-36   Mark 4:2   Mark 4:10-13

B. Distinguish between the first three types of soil in this parable. What is different about the fourth type of soil? *Mark 4:4-8   Mark 4:14-20*

C. The soils represent different sorts of people. Can they also represent different times or influences in your life? *Mark 4:9*

---

69. Colossians 3:2.
70. 1 Peter 1:4.
71. John 3:36.

Chapter 14
Be a light and be a listener

Disc **1** — Track **15**

> **Mark 4:21-25 (NIV)**
> **21** He said to them, "Do you bring in a lamp to put it under a bowl or a bed? Instead, don't you put it on its stand? **22** For whatever is hidden is meant to be disclosed, and whatever is concealed is meant to be brought out into the open. **23** If anyone has ears to hear, let him hear." **24** "Consider carefully what you hear," he continued. "With the measure you use, it will be measured to you—and even more. **25** Whoever has will be given more; whoever does not have, even what he has will be taken from him."

Mark 4:21–23
Light

Jesus talks about buying a lamp and ensuring that everyone sees its light. He says you don't hide a lamp in a bowl or under a bed, but you lift it high on a stand. The light from that lamp reveals whatever the darkness had concealed.

Light chases darkness away. Sin is pictured in the Bible as darkness. That's why when the apostle Paul was converted to Christ, God promised to use him to turn sinners *from darkness to light*.[72] Jesus says twice, *I am the Light of the world*.[73] God's word is also described as a lamp and as a light.[74]

Jesus is *the Light of the world*. When He enters our hearts He chases away sin's darkness within us. That describes Christian conversion. As we read and obey the Bible each day, the ongoing light of God's teaching continues that process. When

---

72. Acts 26:18.
73. John 8:12; John 9:5.
74. Psalm 119:105.

walking in God's light, we enjoy honest and open fellowship with other Christians, and experience the blessing of Christ's blood cleansing us from our sin.[75]

But we also became lighthouses in a dark sin-sick world in danger of judgement for sin. Many ships were saved from shipwreck by lighthouse beams warning about rocks and marking the coastline. As God shines His light in our lives, we will warn others of their need of Christ.[76] We must witness to them by how we live and what we say. The Bible tells us to *Live as children of light.*[77]

Mark 4:23-25

Listen

Jesus then tells us to listen attentively to God. There is important encouragement here if you want to grow in Christ and understand the Bible better. Jesus says you can have as much blessing and understanding as you choose to take. His offer is unlimited. The more you listen to His word and act on it, the more understanding and blessing He gives. He says, *With the measure you use, it will be measured to you—and even more.* There is no excuse for ongoing ignorance of the Bible! Read it a lot (or hear it read if reading is a problem) and pray much about it. God will give you increased light from His word as you take in more and more. Spend time in God's word! Don't skimp your daily intake of it. Take every opportunity to hear the Bible preached and taught. Otherwise your understanding of it and blessing from it will diminish.

Jesus' summary is, *Whoever has will be given more; whoever does not have, even what he has will be taken from him.* Be ambitious for God. Ask Him to increase your love for His word and to help you to follow it. Hunger for God and thirst for His word. He will continue to give you more and more light and blessing from it!

---

75. 1 John 1:7.
76. Matthew 5:16.
77. Ephesians 5:8.

Questions on Chapter 14
Mark 4:21-25 Be a light and be a listener.

A. How does the concept of light help you to understand Jesus and the Bible? *John 8:12   Psalm 119:105*

B. How should light feature in the walk and witness of a committed Christian? *Ephesians 5:8   1 John 1:7*

C. Why does blessing come to those who humbly listen to God through the Bible being preached or taught, and through reading the Bible each day? *2 Timothy 3:16-17   Proverbs 30:5   Psalm 119:9-16*

Chapter 15
The kingdom of God

Mark 4:26-34 (NIV)
[26] He also said, "This is what the kingdom of God is like. A man scatters seed on the ground. [27] Night and day, whether he sleeps or gets up, the seed sprouts and grows, though he does not know how. [28] All by itself the soil produces corn— first the stalk, then the ear, then the full grain in the ear. [29] As soon as the grain is ripe, he puts the sickle to it, because the harvest has come." [30] Again he said, "What shall we say the kingdom of God is like, or what parable shall we use to describe it? [31] It is like a mustard seed, which is the smallest seed you plant in the ground. [32] Yet when planted, it grows and becomes the largest of all garden plants, with such big branches that the birds of the air can perch in its shade." [33] With many similar parables Jesus spoke the word to them, as much as they could understand. [34] He did not say anything to them without using a parable. But when he was alone with his own disciples, he explained everything.

Mark 4:26-34
How does God's kingdom come?

We have seen that the Kingdom of God has come! Jesus came as a human being to Bethlehem and thus to this world. The Kingdom will come when Jesus returns in glory as King of kings and Lord of lords. Meanwhile it does come whenever someone yields to the Saviour/King. Jesus here teaches His kingdom comes as the seed of God's word is sown. It is sown through gospel preaching, Bible teaching and through personal witness to Christ's saving power.

Jesus teaches that God's kingdom comes as when a man scatters seed on the ground or plants a mustard seed.

Mark 4:26-32
How does God's kingdom grow?

Jesus tells two parables demonstrating the growth of God's kingdom. We have already considered the parable of the soils. The other covers planting mustard seed. Putting them together we learn about kingdom growth in five ways.

First, when God's word takes hold of an individual or a nation, it grows **continually**. Jesus says it grows *Night and day*. Secondly, initially it grows **invisibly**. No-one but God knows it is growing. Sometimes God's early work in the life of a guilty sinner is not even realised by the person concerned. Third, its growth is **ordered and definite**. There is an ordered sequence before the seed becomes grain for harvesting. God makes guilty sinners recognise their sin, turn from it to Christ who died for them, and yield their lives to Him to forgive them and to take over in His reign of love and truth. Progress in Christ is through the Holy Spirit's work. Fourth, its growth is **gradual**. Seed planted on Friday morning is not seen growing on Friday afternoon![78] Fifth, the ultimate change is **immense**! As God works in our lives to bring us to His forgiveness we change from lost Hell-bound rebels into saved Heaven-bound Christians!

Mark 4:33-34
How is God's kingdom understood?

Jesus continues to use parables to explain God's truths to as many as can understand. (Christian speakers should make complicated things simple, rather than simple things complicated, though we fail at times!) But note Jesus' prime concern is that His disciples understand Him! He wants His followers to grow in His truth. He accomplishes these aims by spending time alone with them: *when He was alone with His own disciples, He explained everything.*

---

78. In 2 Peter 3:18 the Christian is told to grow—not to jump—in grace and knowledge!

Jesus values highly time spent alone with His disciples, considering His word. His followers today now must also spend time alone with Him and listen to Him through His word![79]

Questions on Chapter 15
Mark 4:26-34 The kingdom of God.

A. In what sense has God's kingdom already come? In what sense is it here now? In what sense will it come in the future? *Matthew 2:1   John 19:3   John 19:19-22   Romans 14:17   Colossians 1:12   1 Timothy 6:13-16-17   Revelation 19:11-16*

B. Using the illustration of seed that Jesus uses, how does God's kingdom grow? *Mark 4:26-29*

C. What should you pray in order to understand God's word better? Can you do anything else to help your understanding of the Bible? *Luke 10:38-42   1 Corinthians 2:12-14*

---

79.   2 Timothy 2:15, 2 Timothy 3:16.

Chapter 16
Two kinds of fear

Mark 4:35-41 (NIV)
[35] That day when evening came, he said to his disciples, "Let us go over to the other side." [36] Leaving the crowd behind, they took him along, just as he was, in the boat. There were also other boats with him. [37] A furious squall came up, and the waves broke over the boat, so that it was nearly swamped. [38] Jesus was in the stern, sleeping on a cushion. The disciples woke him and said to him, "Teacher, don't you care if we drown?" [39] He got up, rebuked the wind and said to the waves, "Quiet! Be still!" Then the wind died down and it was completely calm. [40] He said to his disciples, "Why are you so afraid? Do you still have no faith?" [41] They were terrified and asked each other, "Who is this? Even the wind and the waves obey him!"

Mark 4:35–36
The setting

It is evening. Jesus, with His disciples on Galilee's shore, wants to cross to the other side. Leaving the crowd, they make for the other side by boat. Other boats accompany them. Galilee's sudden windstorms, like whirlwinds, produce near hurricane conditions. Jesus' disciples will face the same stormy condition as the other boats, but Jesus is in the boat with them. Similarly today, Christian disciples face the same problems and troubles as others, but Jesus is always with those who trust Him, even in frightening situations.[80]

---

80. Hebrews 13:5-6.

Mark 4:37-38
Facing the storm-sleeping or scared?

The whirlwind hits the lake. The disciples' boat is swamped and nearly sinking. The Lord of creation, Jesus Christ, sleeps in the stern on a pillow! His panic-stricken disciples wake Him and demand, *Do You not care that we are perishing?* [81]Although wrong to panic with Jesus present, they are completely right to pour out their fears to Him. Christians should always pray like that.[82] Of course Jesus cares! He is our sovereign God. His timetable for us is perfect. He makes no mistakes!

Mark 4: 39
Simple words and stilled waves

Jesus rises and tells the whirlwind to stop! His simple command to the mountainous waves is *Quiet! Be still!* The windstorm stops. The waves disappear. All is calm. We all face storms in our lives. Waves of frightening circumstances, caused by ourselves or by others, seem about to overwhelm us—and sometimes we feel literally help-less. Fearful, we lose our peace. But in knowing Jesus personally we know any storm encountered is under His control and will not last a second longer than is necessary for us. Sometimes those storms are sent to remove our self-centred reliance and teach us to trust God more.

Anyone who has asked Jesus for forgiveness, trusting in His death on the cross and in His powerful indwelling resurrection life within, knows they will avoid judgement's massive storm by that personal faith in Christ. When God judges sins eternally Christians are safely at peace because Jesus bore their sins and punishment on the cross of Calvary! No condemnation remains for such people![83] Eternal peace with God results from that![84]

---

81. NKJV translates the Greek better. NIV paraphrases by the words *don't you care if we drown?*
82. 1 Peter 5:7.
83. Romans 8:1.
84. Philippians 4:6-7.

Mark 4:40–41
Silenced and staggered

The disciples cannot answer Jesus' questions, *Why are you so afraid?* and *Do you still have no faith?* How irrational—for us as well as for them—not to trust fully such a powerful and caring Saviour. Nevertheless Jesus saves them from the storm! He does care! They are rightly staggered in asking, *Who is this? Even the wind and the waves obey Him!* Reverent and justified fear of who He is replaces the tempest's terror. Psalms and Proverbs comment *The fear of the LORD is the beginning of wisdom.*[85]

Questions on Chapter 16
Mark 4:35–41 Two kinds of fear.

A. Why are the disciples frightened in the storm? How is life sometimes like a storm? *Mark 4:40 2 Corinthians 7:5*

B. What difference does it make to the disciples when Jesus calms the storm? How does Jesus do it? *Mark 4:39 John 14:27 Romans 5:1 Colossians 1:20*

C. What does this passage reveal about the Lord Jesus Christ? Does that encourage you to trust Him? *Colossians 1:22-24 2 Peter 1:6 Revelation 5:12*

---

85. Psalm 111:10; Proverbs 9:10.

Chapter 17
From the tombs to tranquility

Disc 2 – Track 01

Mark 5:1-20 (NASB)

¹ And they came to the other side of the sea, into the country of the Gerasenes. ² And when He had come out of the boat, immediately a man from the tombs with an unclean spirit met Him, ³ and he had his dwelling among the tombs. And no one was able to bind him anymore, even with a chain; ⁴ because he had often been bound with shackles and chains, and the chains had been torn apart by him, and the shackles broken in pieces, and no one was strong enough to subdue him. ⁵ And constantly night and day, among the tombs and in the mountains, he was crying out and gashing himself with stones. ⁶ And seeing Jesus from a distance, he ran up and bowed down before Him; ⁷ and crying out with a loud voice, he said, "What do I have to do with You, Jesus, Son of the Most High God? I implore You by God, do not torment me!" ⁸ For He had been saying to him, "Come out of the man, you unclean spirit!" ⁹ And He was asking him, "What is your name?" And he said to Him, "My name is Legion; for we are many." ¹⁰ And he began to entreat Him earnestly not to send them out of the country. ¹¹ Now there was a big herd of swine feeding there on the mountain. ¹² And the demons entreated Him, saying, "Send us into the swine so that we may enter them." ¹³ And He gave them permission. And coming out, the unclean spirits entered the swine; and the herd rushed down the steep bank into the sea, about two thousand of them; and they were drowned in the sea. ¹⁴ And their herdsmen ran away and reported it in the city and out in the country. And the people came to see what it was that had happened. ¹⁵ And they came to Jesus and observed the man who had been demon-possessed sitting down, clothed and in his right mind, the very man who had had the "legion"; and they became frightened. ¹⁶ And those who had seen it described to them how it had happened to the demon-possessed man, and all about the swine. ¹⁷ And they began to entreat Him to depart from their region. ¹⁸ And as He was getting into the boat, the man who had been demon-possessed was entreating Him that he might accompany Him. ¹⁹ And He did not let him, but He said to him, "Go home to your people and report to them

what great things the Lord has done for you, and how He had mercy on you." **20** And he went away and began to proclaim in Decapolis what great things Jesus had done for him; and everyone marvelled.

Mark 5:1-8
A desperate man's despair

On Galilee's eastern shore, influenced by the city of Gadara, is countryside surrounding a small town called Gersa. Jesus travels there by boat. Among the tombs lives a totally uncontrolled man, possessed by an *unclean spirit*. Untameable and strong, he breaks his metal chains, continually shrieks loudly among the mountains and tombs, and gashes himself with stones. Not realising that Jesus can meet his huge need, he runs to Jesus, bows before Him and yells out, *What business do we have with each other, Jesus, Son of the Most High God? I implore You by God, do not torment me!* Despairing of help or healing from the only One who can change him, he fears irrationally that Jesus will harm him. Today, many folks desperately needing Jesus think following Him will spoil and harm their lives. Desperation and despair should drive them to Jesus, not from Him! But Jesus is already working in this man. He commands the unclean spirit to leave this dirty, dangerous, despairing and desperate man, so fully at home among the dead.

Mark 5:9-13
Divine power and drowned pigs

The unclean spirit, named 'Legion', consists of many demons. Showing total power over evil, Jesus ejects them, allowing them to enter a herd of about two thousand swine. The pigs charge into the water and drown.

Mark 5:14-17
Profit lost but peace regained

The swineherds quickly publicise this. Curious crowds gather to see a totally changed man, *clothed and in his right mind,* sitting quietly with Jesus. More scared than ever, they ask Jesus to leave. Profits from pigs counts more than restoring lost humanity.

No matter who or how bad, Jesus still saves and changes all who trust Him.[86] Is *your* life out of control? Do *you* hurt inside and lack peace? Do people avoid you because of your lifestyle? Are you 'hopeless' too? Turn to Jesus. Ask Him to enter your life, to forgive you and rule lovingly in your heart with His peace and purity. He can change you from selfish wrongdoing to love Him and spend time with Him in prayer and Bible reading. But expect some opposition. Some will misunderstand Christ's change in you and think you're strange.[87]

Mark 5: 18–20
New Person–New Priorities

As Jesus is leaving, His new follower asks to accompany Him. Jesus refuses—he must now go tell his own people how God has renewed him. He obeys. In Decapolis he shares with amazed people how Jesus has changed him. What an excellent example for Christians to follow! First trust in Jesus: your life begins to change. Then spend time with Him in personal devotions. Then share the good news with others!

Questions on Chapter 17
Mark 5:1–20 From the tombs to tranquillity.

A. Describe the man who is possessed by the demons. Are there people today who share some of his problems? *Mark 5:2-5 1 John 5:19 Romans 7:19 John 8:34*

B. Contrast the attitudes to Jesus of the totally changed man and those wanting Jesus to leave. What makes the difference? *Isaiah 53:3 Mark 5:17-18 Psalm 116:1*

C. What is the first thing that Jesus asks His new follower to do? What does he actually do? What should you do that perhaps he failed do? How can you do what he rightly did? *Mark 5:18 Mark 5:19-20 Romans 10:9-10*

---

86. Hebrews 7:25.
87. 1 Peter 4:4.

Chapter 18
The need for patience

Disc 2– Track 02

Mark 5:21-27 (NASB)
[21] **And when Jesus had crossed over again in the boat to the other side, a great multitude gathered about Him; and He stayed by the seashore.** [22] **And one of the synagogue officials named Jairus came up, and upon seeing Him, fell at His feet,** [23] **and entreated Him earnestly, saying, "My little daughter is at the point of death; please come and lay Your hands on her, that she may get well and live."** [24] **And He went off with him; and a great multitude was following Him and pressing in on Him.** [25] **And a woman who had had a haemorrhage for twelve years,** [26] **and had endured much at the hands of many physicians, and had spent all that she had and was not helped at all, but rather had grown worse,** [27] **after hearing about Jesus, came up in the crowd behind Him, and touched His cloak.**

Mark 5:21–23
What is real prayer?

Jesus is never off duty.[88] Somebody always needs Him. He works 24/7 to bless those coming to Him. He crosses Galilee again by boat, to be surrounded by a multitude. Unsurprisingly, someone who becomes a serving Christian finds he or she is surrounded by different needs of many people. Life gets very busy, tiring and challenging. However, such service blesses those helped, encourages the helpers by God's help and presence, and glorifies God.

On the shore a synagogue official, Jairus, awaits Jesus. Ignoring his status, he falls at Jesus' feet to plead urgently for his dying little daughter. He yearns that Jesus will

---

88. One of God's attributes is that He is always awake and alert. See Psalm 121:4.

save her. Such a sense of urgency, humility and reliance on Jesus only, mark out real prayer.

Jairus earnestly begs Jesus to answer his very focused and specific prayer. We too need to pray like that. God does not always answer as we want: we don't receive immediately what we request. God delays His answer. Other times He answers 'No'.[89] But God sometimes gives us an unexpected answer far better than we dreamed! Jairus prays for his little twelve year old girl.[90] He begs Jesus, *Please come and lay your hands on her, so that she will get well and live.* We should pray for individual people, family members, sick people, and for youngsters and older folks. Pray whether or not the situation seems hopeless. Place everything in God's loving hands.

Mark 5:24–27
Encouraging immediate response— then frustrating delay

Jairus must be encouraged when Jesus goes with him immediately. Another following crowd engulfs Jesus. Jairus hopes for a wonderful miracle for his twelve year old daughter. Jesus has often immediately and permanently cured other sufferers! Surely Jairus will soon see Jesus save his daughter? Sometimes we rejoice in immediate answers to prayer. But sometimes what starts positively seems to get ambushed and complicated. We can become emotionally frustrated, sad, and even angry. But that will not bring answered prayer. We must continue following Jesus and pray for His will.[91]

Jairus is now upstaged when a woman with a serious and long term haemorrhage approaches Jesus. Her illness started the year Jairus' daughter was born. For the past twelve years Jairus' daughter has been growing up whilst the woman has moved nearer to death. Now death beckons the girl and healthy living seems possible for the woman. After years of fruitless medical treatment she seizes her opportunity to

---

89. This can be because we are living in rebellion to God or ask for the wrong thing. See James 4:2.
90. Mark 5:42.
91. 1 Thessalonians 5:17.

seek Christ's help. Jesus stops. Jairus' heart must now be in his mouth: 'What about my dying daughter?' he must think.

We need God's patience to accept God's will in God's time.[92] But keep 'tuned'! We will meet Jairus again soon! Jesus forgets no-one who prays to Him—and that includes you!

Questions on Chapter 18
Mark 5:21–27 The need for patience.

A. **Compare the basic needs of Jairus with your own. Are the basic needs of prominent people in society basically different from the needs of 'ordinary' people?** Romans 3:23   Hebrews 9:27   Romans 3:10   Romans 10:12-13

B. **What do you think encourages Jairus initially? How will that encouragement be tested soon?** Mark 5:24   Mark 5:27   Hebrews 6:12

C. **Compare the concerns of the sick woman with that of Jairus' daughter. How are they similar and how are they different?** Mark 5:23   Mark 5:25-27   Psalm 145:18   Isaiah 55:6

---

92.   James 1:3. In this verse *endurance* includes 'patience' as we know it.

Chapter 19
Brushing by Jesus or touching Him in faith?

Mark 5:25-34 (NASB)
25 And a woman who had had a haemorrhage for twelve years, 26 and had endured much at the hands of many physicians, and had spent all that she had and was not helped at all, but rather had grown worse, 27 after hearing about Jesus, came up in the crowd behind Him, and touched His cloak. 28 For she thought, "If I just touch His garments, I shall get well." 29 And immediately the flow of her blood was dried up; and she felt in her body that she was healed of her affliction. 30 And immediately Jesus, perceiving in Himself that the power proceeding from Him had gone forth, turned around in the crowd and said, "Who touched My garments?" 31 And His disciples said to Him, "You see the multitude pressing in on You, and You say, 'Who touched Me?'" 32 And He looked around to see the woman who had done this. 33 But the woman fearing and trembling, aware of what had happened to her, came and fell down before Him, and told Him the whole truth. 34 And He said to her, "Daughter, your faith has made you well; go in peace, and be healed of your affliction."

Mark 5:25–26
Sensing the need for Jesus

A needy woman with a twelve year long haemorrhage approaches Jesus, en route with Jairus to see his dying daughter. She has spent all her money on many doctors and 'quacks', yet without cure. Her health has deteriorated. She gets older, sicker and nearer death.

Mark 5:27-28
Putting personal faith in Jesus

Others told her about Jesus. (It is important to tell others that Christ can save.[93]) The woman is now in the crowd. She really believes Jesus can meet her need. She says to herself, *If I just touch His garments, I will get well.* But believing Jesus can heal falls short of asking Him to do it.

She now touches His cloak in a deliberate act of personal faith. She knows her need, believes Jesus can meet it, and effectively asks Him to do so by touching His cloak. While many brush by Jesus, her touch is like a direct prayer to Him.

Mark 5:29-34
Restoration, challenge, assurance and peace

Remember that Mark's Gospel often deals with things happening *immediately*. Three cases of *immediately* follow! Jesus meets her need for restoration *immediately*. She knows *immediately* that Jesus heals her. Jesus knows *immediately* that power from Him heals her. When any guilty sinner places personal faith in Christ's atoning death on Calvary, *immediately* that person is saved and receives eternal life.[94]

Now Jesus challenges: *Who touched My garments?* He knows the answer but encourages her to confess to others that she is trusting Him. The disciples cannot distinguish between the crowd's brushing by Jesus and the needy woman's personal trusting Him through her touch. Many brush by Jesus in history, religion, paintings, poems, and even by observing today's date, testifying that Jesus split time into 'BC' and 'AD'. But knowing **about** Jesus is different from coming to know Him by personally receiving Him within as personal risen and living Lord and Saviour.

The woman meets Christ's challenge, though *fearing and trembling.* She publicly declares to Jesus before everyone that she touched His cloak as her personal act of faith. Jesus assures her that He really has restored her, and calls this new child

---

93. Romans 10:14.
94. 1 John 5:12-13.

of God *'Daughter'*. He says *Daughter, your faith has made you well.* His promise of peace follows: *go in peace and be healed of your affliction.*

You can also cease to brush by Jesus superficially. Recognise Jesus' death on the cross is for you. He carried God's judgement for your sins and rose again to become your Saviour. Then ask Him to forgive you and enter your life. Two wonderful things follow: first, you can be certain of having eternal life; [95] second you receive peace with God through Christ's shed blood. [96] His peace increasingly rules your heart through your indwelling Saviour [97] and by the Holy Spirit's work in you.

Questions on Chapter 19
Mark 5:25–34 Brushing by Jesus or touching Him in faith?

A. Why can the woman with the haemorrhage be optimistic? But what may hinder her from coming to Jesus? *Mark 3:7-11   Mark 5:20   Mark 5:24-26.*

B. In how many ways can you see that Jesus is in control? *Mark 5: 3-34*

C. What is the difference between the woman's touching Jesus' cloak and the people's just brushing past Him? What does the woman's trust in Jesus produce? *Mark 5:27-28   Mark 5:31   Hebrews 11:6*

---

95. 1 John 5:13.
96. Colossians 1:20.
97. Colossians 3:15.

Chapter 20
Unfinished business

> **Mark 5:35-43 (NASB)**
> ³⁵ While He was still speaking, they came from the house of the synagogue official, saying, "Your daughter has died; why trouble the Teacher anymore?" ³⁶ But Jesus, overhearing what was being spoken, said to the synagogue official, "Do not be afraid any longer, only believe." ³⁷ And He allowed no one to follow with Him, except Peter and James and John the brother of James. ³⁸ And they came to the house of the synagogue official; and He beheld a commotion, and people loudly weeping and wailing. ³⁹ And entering in, He said to them, "Why make a commotion and weep? The child has not died, but is asleep." ⁴⁰ And they began laughing at Him. But putting them all out, He took along the child's father and mother and His own companions, and entered the room where the child was. ⁴¹ And taking the child by the hand, He said to her, "Talitha kum!" (which translated means, "Little girl, I say to you, arise!"). ⁴² And immediately the girl rose and began to walk; for she was twelve years old. And immediately they were completely astounded. ⁴³ And He gave them strict orders that no one should know about this; and He said that something should be given her to eat.

Mark 5:35
Too late?

Does Jairus despairingly think, 'My darling little daughter is probably dead by now.'? If so, his worst fears are confirmed by messengers from his home: *Your daughter has died*. So why bother Jesus now? What a tragic disappointment! Does Jairus wonder if Jesus spoiled everything a by stopping to heal the woman with the haemorrhage?

Mark 5:36–40
Christ in control

But Jesus is never too late and never too early. His timing is always perfect. Remember that when things are going 'pear shaped'. He overhears the words to Jairus. He tells Jairus to stop fearing, but believe in Him. Then He gathers His inner cabinet of Peter, James and John. He does not need them, but their faith will be strengthened in Him. He tells the wailing mourners not to make a *commotion and weep*. They ridicule Him when He says, *The child has not died, but is asleep.*

Death in the Bible, is the separation of body from soul. Eternal death, or Hell, is the separation of body and soul from God forever in punishment.[98] Jesus holds the keys of life and death, and eternity as the Sovereign Lord.[99] Yes, Jairus' daughter is physically dead. But Jesus will reverse nature, which He controls, and turn death into sleep from which He will wake her safely in His own way!

Jesus excludes the mocking mourners. They seem to be paid professionals rather than genuine family friends concerned for the girl. Jesus takes the girl's parents with Peter, James and John into her bedroom.

Mark 5:41–43
Alive and fed

The conclusion of this episode is majestically predictable! Jesus brings the little girl to life. He does this simply by His words *Talitha kum!* which mean *Little girl, I say to you, get up!* Again we see the life-giving power of the word of God, and of the Lord Jesus Christ.[100] He then takes the child *by the hand*. She walks. Jesus excludes the curious sensation-seekers. No-one else joins the five chosen people. He demonstrates His practical concern for her by making sure she is fed! Jesus is loving, caring, powerful, and mightily in control—but He is also 'down to earth'.

Those who trust the promises of the Bible (God's written word) and put their trust

---

98. Romans 1:18; Ephesians 5:6.
99. Jesus said that all power had been given to Him. See Matthew 28:18.
100. Hebrews 4:12.

the Lord Jesus (God's living word) receive eternal life from Him. He deals with all of us—from the youngest to the oldest—with great personal care and love. What a marvellous Saviour we have!

Questions on Chapter 20
Mark 5:35–43 Unfinished business.

A. How does Jairus respond when he hears discouraging news? How should you respond to discouragement? *Mark 5:35 Mark 9:22-24 1 Samuel 30:6 Isaiah 40:31*

B. Trace Jesus' absolute control through His words and actions. *Mark 5:36, 39 & 41*

C. What blend of divine power and practical caring does Jesus demonstrate in restoring Jairus' daughter? *Mark 5:41 Luke 5:17*

Chapter 21
Rejected at home

> **Mark 6:1-6 (NASB)**
> [1] And He went out from there, and He came into His home town; and His disciples followed Him. [2] And when the Sabbath had come, He began to teach in the synagogue; and the many listeners were astonished, saying, "Where did this man get these things, and what is this wisdom given to Him, and such miracles as these performed by His hands? [3] "Is not this the carpenter, the son of Mary, and brother of James, and Joses, and Judas, and Simon? Are not His sisters here with us?" And they took offense at Him. [4] And Jesus said to them, "A prophet is not without honor except in his home town and among his own relatives and in his own household." [5] And He could do no miracle there except that He laid His hands upon a few sick people and healed them. [6] And He wondered at their unbelief. And He was going around the villages teaching.

Mark 6:1-3
Local reaction to Jesus

If you have ever been rejected unfairly at home take comfort that Jesus has been there before you. He knows exactly how that feels. He never did anything to deserve such treatment. By comparison we are rarely, if ever, completely blameless.

Jesus' disciples follow Him to His Nazareth home. He teaches in the synagogue on the Sabbath. His wise words and powerful miracles make people question the source of His wisdom and power. Sincere questioning can help the questioners to trust Christ, whose wisdom and power are divine.[101] But prejudiced people don't want correct answers, but they want to justify their prejudices. One rhyme suggests

---

101. 1 Corinthians 1:24.

'A man convinced against His will is of the same opinion still!'

So the people belittle Jesus, referring to Him as *the carpenter* (his stepfather's trade) and as *the son of Mary* in innuendos about His illegitimacy. (Ungodly people misunderstand the fact of and the reason for His miraculous virgin birth). In mocking Jesus, they imply He is no different from his physical brothers and sisters. They see Jesus as a jumped-up upstart parading as a 'somebody'. To them he is a 'nobody' from a 'nowhere town'.

Mark 6:4-6
The response of Jesus

Jesus responds to this opposition and coldness by revealing a true understanding of human nature, and encouraging Christian preachers today when opposed by those nearest to them. Christ teaches that God's messengers may be honoured by many but heavily opposed when at home. Relatives and close family may well be antagonistic.

But even so, Jesus wonders *at their unbelief* and their excessive opposition to Him at home. Perhaps His perfect holiness offends them? Unlike them, He always pleases the Father, making them see their own sin very clearly. Resentment can be for two very different reasons. Either a bad, hypocritical reputation causes opposition, or alternatively, as with Jesus, a good reputation evokes envy and jealousy, stifling justified praise and resulting in evil and malicious taunting. When our sinfulness is highlighted by Christ's spotlessness, we either turn from our sins and receive God's forgiveness or harden our hearts to oppose God's message and messengers.[102]

God works in us by grace in response to personal faith.[103] Those trusting Him know He is working in their and other lives through that 'amazing grace.' But here unbelief of some, familiar with Jesus since infancy, prevents much blessing. Unbelief always blocks blessing. No one comes to Christ while unbelievingly rejecting God's word. We must demonstrate faith in God and the Bible's promises by trusting and obeying Him.[104]

---

102. Just as John 1:11 records about Jesus.
103. Ephesians 2:8-9.
104. Hebrews 11:6.

Jesus now works only a few miracles in Nazareth. He heals a few sick people, however. Even amidst opposition and unbelief, some are blessed in trusting Him! Jesus doesn't give up because of opposition at home. Not at all! He is *going around the villages teaching*. He has a top priority job to do, teaching God's word!

Understanding and trusting God's word causes men and women to be saved. Observing miracles cannot save. They simply signify who the Saviour is. Hearing God's word is a priority for all, and teaching it for some.

Questions on Chapter 21
Mark 6:1-6 Rejected at home.

A. Why are the people in Jesus' home town offended by Him? Mark 6:2-3 Mark 6:4

B. How can we deal with opposition in a way that honours God and blesses our family, and even our enemies? Mark 6:4 Matthew 5:44

C. How can unbelief affect God's working in our lives? How should we handle unbelief? Mark 6:5 Mark 16:14 Mark 9:24

Chapter 22
Serving in God's team

Disc Track
2 – 06

Mark 6:7-13 (NASB)
⁷ And He summoned the twelve and began to send them out in pairs; and He was giving them authority over the unclean spirits; ⁸ and He instructed them that they should take nothing for their journey, except a mere staff; no bread, no bag, no money in their belt; ⁹ but to wear sandals; and He added, "Do not put on two tunics." ¹⁰ And He said to them, "Wherever you enter a house, stay there until you leave town. ¹¹ "And any place that does not receive you or listen to you, as you go out from there, shake off the dust from the soles of your feet for a testimony against them." ¹² And they went out and preached that men should repent. ¹³ And they were casting out many demons and were anointing with oil many sick people and healing them.

Mark 6:7–11
Jesus calls His twelve apostles

'Apostle' means someone who is sent. Jesus now calls and sends His twelve apostles to preach and teach His message. They will perform special tasks, never to be repeated in history. God's Holy Spirit will inspire them and their close associates to write the New Testament, thus completing God's written word, the Bible. Earlier God's Holy Spirit moved men to write the Old Testament.[105] The whole true Christian church will be built on God's self-revelation through them. Jesus will identify them to their hearers as God's apostles by miraculous signs. They will be His unique messengers laying the foundation of the New Testament church.

Right now, Jesus sends out the apostles in twos and empowers them to cast out

---
105. 2 Peter 1:21.

unclean spirits. They will be noticed as they share God's word. They must carry minimum baggage and only take a staff, useful for walking or protection from wild animals or mad dogs. They must take no bread, bag, money, change of clothing, or strong shoes—only sandals. They are to assess their hearers' response by the hospitality offered to them. Those receiving God's word will welcome them into their homes. When unwelcome they must shake the dust from their feet to warn their rejecters of the grave danger of not responding to God's word. Unless there is real repentance eternal judgement will follow.[106] Perhaps the dramatic act of shaking the dust from their feet will cause some, to think, repent, and turn to God later?

Mark 6:12-13
The twelve apostles go out to preach

At Jesus' command the apostles go out and preach. They pass on His message, namely that God commands sinners to *repent*. Repentance means being so sorry for disobeying God and hurting others that you ask for His forgiveness, deliberately turning your back on everything wrong in your life. Repentance becomes a pattern to continue to follow by God's grace and help. If you repent and trust Jesus as your Saviour, you surrender your right to go your own sinful way. From now on you will accept His Lordship over how you live your life in the future. Repentance is like leaving a train going in the wrong direction, in order to catch one going to the right destination. You leave your sinful ways and ask God to help you follow Him. God demands that attitude of repentance in order to cleanse you from your sins and enter your life as your Lord and Saviour. Because Jesus took your condemnation and death sentence on Himself and rose again, you receive His risen life and live for Him. One day you will spend eternity with Him in Heaven.[107]

As the apostles go and preach, Jesus' plan is working. They will use Christ's authority and power to cast out demons and heal. Open minded listeners will recognise they speak with divine authority as they speak for Jesus. Today Christian speakers do not perform similar dramatic miracles but demonstrate Christ's authority by preaching God's word, the Bible, in the power of the Holy Spirit. They preach His gospel, which

---

106. Luke 13:3, Luke 13:5.
107. John 14:1-6.

is God's power to save.[108] There is no greater power than that which raises to new and eternal life those who are dead in sin!

Questions on Chapter 22
Mark 6:7-13 Serving in God's team.

A. What advantages can you think of in the twelve disciples going out in pairs to preach, rather than alone? *Mark 6:7   Luke 22:8   Acts 3:1-11   Acts 8:14 Galatians 2:9*

B. How is shaking the dust from the soles of the disciples' feet a testimony against those who will not receive or listen to God's message through them? *Mark 6: 10-12   Matthew 7:6*

C. On what does the preaching of the twelve disciples now focus? What does God enable them to do to demonstrate that they are serving the Son of God in preaching His truth? *Mark 6:12   2 Corinthians 12   Acts 14:3   Acts 4:30 Romans 15:9   Mark 13:21-22   Matthew 16:4*

---

108. Romans 1:16.

Chapter 23
A very sad interlude

Mark 6:14-29 (NASB)

14 And King Herod heard of it, for His name had become well known; and people were saying, "John the Baptist has risen from the dead, and that is why these miraculous powers are at work in Him." 15 But others were saying, "He is Elijah." And others were saying, "He is a prophet, like one of the prophets of old." 16 But when Herod heard of it, he kept saying, "John, whom I beheaded, has risen!" 17 For Herod himself had sent and had John arrested and bound in prison on account of Herodias, the wife of his brother Philip, because he had married her. 18 For John had been saying to Herod, "It is not lawful for you to have your brother's wife." 19 And Herodias had a grudge against him and wanted to put him to death and could not do so; 20 for Herod was afraid of John, knowing that he was a righteous and holy man, and kept him safe. And when he heard him, he was very perplexed; but he used to enjoy listening to him. 21 And a strategic day came when Herod on his birthday gave a banquet for his lords and military commanders and the leading men of Galilee; 22 and when the daughter of Herodias herself came in and danced, she pleased Herod and his dinner guests; and the king said to the girl, "Ask me for whatever you want and I will give it to you." 23 And he swore to her, "Whatever you ask of me, I will give it to you; up to half of my kingdom." 24 And she went out and said to her mother, "What shall I ask for?" And she said, "The head of John the Baptist." 25 And immediately she came in haste before the king and asked, saying, "I want you to give me right away the head of John the Baptist on a platter." 26 And although the king was very sorry, yet because of his oaths and because of his dinner guests, he was unwilling to refuse her. 27 And immediately the king sent an executioner and commanded him to bring back his head. And he went and had him beheaded in the prison, 28 and brought his head on a platter, and gave it to the girl; and the girl gave it to her

mother. [29] **And when his disciples heard about this, they came and took away his body and laid it in a tomb.**

Mark 6:14-29

The staggering reputation of John the Baptist

King Herod hears what Jesus and His disciples are doing. Rumours circulate about who Jesus is—perhaps Elijah or another prophet? Herod thinks Jesus is a resurrected John the Baptist. That cannot be, but it shows John's amazing impact on the wicked king. What a reputation!

Herod had beheaded John when asked by Herodias' daughter. Her daughter pleased Herod and his guests by dancing at Herod's birthday feast One can imagine what kind of dancing they applauded as alcohol flowed. Herod rashly promised to give her up to half his kingdom. Herodias, his immoral mistress and brother's wife, made her request John the Baptist's head on a platter. Herod, too proud to withdraw his promise before his guests, complied despite feeling *very sorry*. How weak!

Herodias hated John the Baptist because he told Herod, *It is not lawful for you to have your brother's wife.* John's brave faithfulness to God's word and standards cost him his life. His example reminds Christians to obey God without compromise, even when threatened by evil. It reminds us that following Jesus can be very costly. Many others have been killed by putting God first. We need God's help and strength to follow Christ, and His special grace to face opposition, if it comes.

Mark 6:29

But where is John the Baptist now?

John's disciples loyally came to collect his body to bury it. Viewed from eternity, all Christians' sufferings are light compared with the weight of glory and blessing ahead in Christ.[109] John's death simply promoted him into Paradise sooner than expected! Paul, writes later to the Philippian Christians that to *be with Christ - - - is*

---
109. 2 Corinthians 4:17.

very much *better.*[110]

All life's gains and losses reduce in importance when considered in the light of eternity. Death makes a millionaire no richer than a bankrupt. A deceased property tycoon is no better off than a beggar dying while sleeping on the street. The world's most popular man has no advantage in death over an unknown hermit. Kings and queens in sumptuous palaces and murderers serving life sentences are on level ground in death.

Without a personal trust in Christ—which alone gives us eternal life[111] instead of our deserved eternal judgement—life is short and rudderless. Knowing Christ as Saviour changes that. With past sins forgiven, our present life is purposeful as we live for Christ in His strength. Our eternal future is secure in Jesus.

Questions on Chapter 23
Mark 6:14–29 A very sad interlude.

A. What about John the Baptist impresses you most? Mark 6:18-20   John 1:19-36

B. What must we expect at times if we insist on applying God's truth rather than on pleasing men? Mark 6:17-19, 27   2 Timothy 3:12

C. Consider the weaknesses of King Herod? Do you have any of those weaknesses? If so, how can God help you overcome them? Mark 6:20 2 Timothy 4:3 Mark 6:22-23 1 John 2:16 Ecclesiastes 5:2 Mark 6:26 Proverbs 29:25 1 John 1:17 James 1:5

---

110. Philippians 1:23.
111. Acts 4:12.

Chapter 24
The master of the miraculous

Disc Track
2 – 08

Mark 6:30-44 (NASB)

[30] And the apostles gathered together with Jesus; and they reported to Him all that they had done and taught. [31] And He said to them, "Come away by yourselves to a lonely place and rest a while." (For there were many people coming and going, and they did not even have time to eat.) [32] And they went away in the boat to a lonely place by themselves. [33] And the people saw them going, and many recognized them, and they ran there together on foot from all the cities, and got there ahead of them. [34] And when He went ashore, He saw a great multitude, and He felt compassion for them because they were like sheep without a shepherd; and He began to teach them many things. [35] And when it was already quite late, His disciples came up to Him and began saying, "The place is desolate and it is already quite late; [36] send them away so that they may go into the surrounding countryside and villages and buy themselves something to eat." [37] But He answered and said to them, "You give them something to eat!" And they said to Him, "Shall we go and spend two hundred denarii on bread and give them something to eat?" [38] And He said to them, "How many loaves do you have? Go look!" And when they found out, they said, "Five and two fish." [39] And He commanded them all to recline by groups on the green grass. [40] And they reclined in companies of hundreds and of fifties. [41] And He took the five loaves and the two fish, and looking up toward heaven, He blessed the food and broke the loaves and He kept giving them to the disciples to set before them; and He divided up the two fish among them all. [42] And they all ate and were satisfied. [43] And they picked up twelve full baskets of the broken pieces, and also of the fish. [44] And there were five thousand men who ate the loaves.

Mark 6:30-34
Report back—and rest?

The twelve apostles report back to Jesus all that they have *done and taught*. It is good to share with Christ our plans to serve Him and afterwards to review our work with him. Then we learn how to improve our service, and thank Him for His help. The twelve meet with Jesus physically. We meet Him spiritually in prayer as our 'Emmanuel' or 'God with us'[112].

Jesus cares for His servants, knowing when they need a rest. His team has no time to eat, so Jesus calls them to rest. They go by boat together, but are recognised and overtaken by crowds who run ahead of them. So much for their rest! Sometimes serving Christ is like that. There is nothing wrong with sometimes taking time out— but others' needs and urgency to share the gospel may mean we can miss out.

Jesus looks compassionately. The large crowd, is *like sheep without a shepherd*. But because they need to receive God's word, Jesus begins *to teach them many things*. Thank God for those who have shared God's word with us and helped us to trust God, know Him better, and understand the Bible.

Mark 6:35-44
Feeding the five thousand

Twice Jesus feeds thousands with very small amounts of food. Here is first time He feeds a large crowd, including five thousand men. As they meet in a remote place and it is late, the disciples ask Jesus to send the people away to buy food. Jesus' staggering reply is *You give them something to eat*. Their reply shows they have insufficient funds to buy the necessary food. Jesus makes them collect any available food. They gather five loaves and two fishes from a lad's lunch pack, according to John's Gospel. [113]. Jesus organises the crowd into *groups of hundreds and fifties*. He blesses and breaks the loaves and divides the fish. His disciples distribute it.

---

112. Matthew 1:23.
113. John 6:9

Everyone eats all they need. Twelve baskets of scraps are gathered!

This miracle reminds us that the Lord Jesus is God the Creator in flesh and that when God works mightily and miraculously, He nethertheless requires good organisation and teamwork. He includes His disciples as He blesses others. Today, many people are starved of the word of God and know little of Jesus, the Bread of Life. [114] Christians should share His word with those who lack understanding of the good news of forgiveness through Jesus. As the gospel message is shared, many people who are hungering for reality and meaning will come to know Christ. They will experience real satisfaction which only Jesus can give—and which expands into perfect blessing in Heaven.

Questions on Chapter 24

Mark 6:30-44 The Master of the miraculous.

A. What happens when Jesus and the disciples go to rest together? What do the actions of the disciples tell you about their attitude? Mark 6:32-24

B. Why does Jesus have compassion on the large crowd? What does He do to help them? Mark 6:34

C. What balance is there here between Jesus' miraculous power, good organisational management, and team work? How should we seek that balance, in following and serving Him? Mark 6:38-41, 43   1 Corinthians 14:40

---

114. John 6:35, John 6:48.

Mark 6:45-56 (NASB)

45 And immediately He made His disciples get into the boat and go ahead of Him to the other side to Bethsaida, while He Himself was sending the multitude away. 46 And after bidding them farewell, He departed to the mountain to pray. 47 And when it was evening, the boat was in the midst of the sea, and He was alone on the land. 48 And seeing them straining at the oars, for the wind was against them, at about the fourth watch of the night, He came to them, walking on the sea; and He intended to pass by them. 49 But when they saw Him walking on the sea, they supposed that it was a ghost, and cried out; 50 for they all saw Him and were frightened. But immediately He spoke with them and said to them, "Take courage; it is I, do not be afraid." 51 And He got into the boat with them, and the wind stopped; and they were greatly astonished, 52 for they had not gained any insight from the incident of the loaves, but their heart was hardened. 53 And when they had crossed over they came to land at Gennesaret, and moored to the shore. 54 And when they had come out of the boat, immediately the people recognized Him, 55 and ran about that whole country and began to carry about on their pallets those who were sick, to the place they heard He was. 56 And wherever He entered villages, or cities, or countryside, they were laying the sick in the market places, and entreating Him that they might just touch the fringe of His cloak; and as many as touched it were being cured.

Mark 6:45–50

Without Jesus in the boat

After feeding the crowd miraculously, Jesus dismisses them. He sends His disciples by boat to Bethsaida while He prays alone on a mountain. Between 3.00 a.m. and 6.00 a.m., His disciples struggle to row the tossing boat in the turbulent sea. Facing a strong head wind, they make little progress. The disciples are terrified when Jesus appears, walking towards them on the water. They cry out. They think He is a ghost! But even before entering the boat Jesus assures them, *Take courage; it is I, do not be afraid.*

Jesus fully understands their situation. He understands their losing struggle to advance against mounting waves as they become exhausted. He knows the fierceness of the wind. Leaving His personal prayer time to walk over the water towards them, He scares them stiff! They panic. Petrified, they cannot distinguish Jesus from a ghost!

Christ's example, to spend time alone with His Father in prayer is one to follow. Serious pray-ers are most able to help others. Sadly, like the disciples: we often struggle in our own strength, and make little progress. We get tired and scared. But take heart! Jesus always knows where to find His followers, whatever their circumstances. He comes to help, wherever we are. Never far away, He encourages us to trust Him and move forward.[115] Like the disciples, we panic and fear when we should trust and obey. But hearing His word encourages us not to fear.

Mark 6:51–52

With Jesus in the boat

A children's song rightly says 'With Christ in the vessel we can smile at the storm.' It is true! Jesus enters the boat. The wind stops! He says nothing to the storm this time—simply He is in absolute control. His disciples are *utterly astonished*. Their dull hearts still fail to recognise His incomparable power, He who so recently fed thousands of people with hardly any food!

115. Hebrews 4:16.

Christ changes the lives amazingly of those trusting Him as Saviour. He changes everything. Yet we can be so slow to remember Who He is and all that He has done for us. Reading the Bible regularly reminds us of Jesus' character, words and deeds, and His presence with us in the boat of our lives.

Mark 6:53–56
The healing touch of Christ

The disciples and Jesus arrive at Gennesaret. They tie up and leave the boat. People from all over recognise Him and come carrying ill people. The same happens in villages, cities and countryside. Like the woman with the haemorrhage previously,[116] all touching his clothes are healed.

Similarly today, everyone who comes to Jesus for forgiveness and eternal life receives them! Have you come to Him?

Questions on Chapter 25
Mark 6:45–56 Jesus walks on water.

A. Contrast Jesus praying in the mountain and the disciples struggling in the boat, battling against the strong wind and sea. *Mark 6:46-48*

B. Are the disciples right to be so astonished and frightened? Should they expect this from Jesus? Do you expect Jesus to help you in the most difficult circumstances? *Mark 6:48-52 Matthew 28:20 Hebrews 4:16*

C. Does Jesus ever fail when He seeks to heal people? Is it more important to have your body healed or to have your eternal soul saved? Why? *Mark 6:56 John 3:16-18, & 36 John 10:28 Mark 8:36 Luke 12:4-5*

---

116. Mark 5:29.

Chapter 26
Hypocrisy and the human heart

Mark 7:1-23 (NASB)

[1] And the Pharisees and some of the scribes gathered together around Him when they had come from Jerusalem, [2] and had seen that some of His disciples were eating their bread with impure hands, that is, unwashed. [3] (For the Pharisees and all the Jews do not eat unless they carefully wash their hands, thus observing the traditions of the elders; [4] and when they come from the market place, they do not eat unless they cleanse themselves; and there are many other things which they have received in order to observe, such as the washing of cups and pitchers and copper pots.) [5] And the Pharisees and the scribes asked Him, "Why do Your disciples not walk according to the tradition of the elders, but eat their bread with impure hands?" [6] And He said to them, "Rightly did Isaiah prophesy of you hypocrites, as it is written, 'THIS PEOPLE HONORS ME WITH THEIR LIPS, BUT THEIR HEART IS FAR AWAY FROM ME. [7] 'BUT IN VAIN DO THEY WORSHIP ME, TEACHING AS DOCTRINES THE PRECEPTS OF MEN.' [8] "Neglecting the commandment of God, you hold to the tradition of men." [9] He was also saying to them, "You nicely set aside the commandment of God in order to keep your tradition. [10] "For Moses said, 'HONOR YOUR FATHER AND YOUR MOTHER'; and, 'HE WHO SPEAKS EVIL OF FATHER OR MOTHER, LET HIM BE PUT TO DEATH'; [11] but you say, 'If a man says to his father or his mother, anything of mine you might have been helped by is Corban (that is to say, given to God),' [12] you no longer permit him to do anything for his father or his mother; [13] thus invalidating the word of God by your tradition which you have handed down; and you do many things such as that." [14] And after He called the multitude to Him again, He began saying to them, "Listen to Me, all of you, and understand: [15] there is nothing outside the man which going into him can defile him; but the things which proceed out of the man are what defile the man. [16] "If any man has ears to hear, let him hear." [17] And when leaving the multitude, He had entered the house, His disciples questioned Him about the parable. [18] And He said to them, "Are you so lacking in

understanding also? Do you not understand that whatever goes into the man from outside cannot defile him; [19] because it does not go into his heart, but into his stomach, and is eliminated? "(Thus He declared all foods clean.) [20] And He was saying, "That which proceeds out of the man, that is what defiles the man. [21] "For from within, out of the heart of men, proceed the evil thoughts, fornications, thefts, murders, adulteries, [22] deeds of coveting and wickedness, as well as deceit, sensuality, envy, slander, pride and foolishness. [23] "All these evil things proceed from within and defile the man."

Mark 7:1-13

What is a hypocrite?

The word 'hypocrisy' historically described an actor. It means 'play acting'. A 'hypocrite' pretends to be someone else. Jesus here criticises some religious people—the Pharisees and some scribes—for this. They appear very religious in deeds and words, but their hearts are far from God. They concentrate on outward ceremonies—including set routines for ceremonially washing hands, pots and utensils. This is not for hygiene, but for show to impress others. They deny God's word while pretending to follow it, trying to appear to honour Him.[117] Their traditions ignore and oppose God's word. One tradition concerns treating needy parents. The Bible insists parents must be honoured and spoken of respectfully. But they refuse to support financially needy mothers and fathers claiming that the money has been given to God instead. That supposed gift to God is called 'Corban'.

God hates hypocrisy. It prevents people being forgiven and put in right relationship with Him. The hypocrite's sham involves refusing to admit culpability and the need of forgiveness. This prevents hypocrites coming to God through Christ for forgiveness and cleansing. Hypocrites should 'get real', confess their sin to God, forsake it, and ask Jesus to forgive it and enter their hearts and lives. Christ will always forgive and change repentant hypocrites!

Mark 7:14-23

The human heart

Jesus teaches our real problem is that we are rebel sinners against God. We have

---

117. Isaiah 29:13 shows this was not a new problem. Cf Mark 7:6.

wicked hearts.[118] Morally, like sewers, they contain within a nature against God that is filthy in sin. We are not defiled by outward things—such as what we eat—but by the evil selfishness from our wicked and deceitful hearts.

But we can receive God's needed cleansing within[119] through Christ's death on the cross. All the filth of our sin was poured on Him there as He took God the Father's punishment for it in our place.[120] He rose again! Christ comes through the indwelling Holy Spirit to live in our repentant hearts by faith.[121] Our hearts then start to change and respond to God and His word, in a new relationship with God.

Here is the depressing list that Jesus gives of what comes out of our hearts: *evil thoughts, fornications* [meaning acts of sexual immorality], *thefts, murder, adulteries, deeds of coveting and wickedness, as well as deceit, sensuality, envy, slander, pride and foolishness.* Yet all of these sins are forgiven us, when we repent of them and put our personal trust in Jesus Christ? 1 John 1:7 says: *the blood of Jesus Christ, God's Son, cleanses us from **all** sin.*[122]

When Jesus saves someone, that person receives His cleansing and starts knowing the Holy Spirit's controlling influence in the heart. By God's grace deceitful hypocrisy begins to decline and progressively an open and honest person begins to emerge. Does that describe you?

Questions on Chapter 26

Mark 7:1-23 Hypocrisy and the human heart

A. How does the refusal of the Pharisees and some of the Scribes to support needy parents show that they are hypocrites? *Mark 7:6-16*

B. What evil comes from the human heart? How can such a filthy heart be cleansed and changed by God? *Mark 7:15, 20-21 1 John 1:7-9 Psalm 51:10*

C. Why is it vitally important to deal with the heart first rather than with external matters? *Mark 7:20 Jeremiah 17:9 Jeremiah 29:13*

---

118. Jeremiah 17:9.
119. Psalm 51:10.
120. Isaiah 53:4-6, 1Peter 2:24.
121. Ephesians 3:17.
122. NASB, like NKJV, translates it thus. NIV uses *purifies* instead of *cleanses*.

Chapter 27
Dealing with outsiders

Mark 7:24-37 (NASB)
24 And from there He arose and went away to the region of Tyre. And when He had entered a house, He wanted no one to know of it; yet He could not escape notice. 25 But after hearing of Him, a woman whose little daughter had an unclean spirit, immediately came and fell at His feet. 26 Now the woman was a Gentile, of the Syrophoenician race. And she kept asking Him to cast the demon out of her daughter. 27 And He was saying to her, "Let the children be satisfied first, for it is not good to take the children's bread and throw it to the dogs." 28 But she answered and said to Him, "Yes, Lord, but even the dogs under the table feed on the children's crumbs." 29 And He said to her, "Because of this answer go your way; the demon has gone out of your daughter." 30 And going back to her home, she found the child lying on the bed, the demon having departed.

31 And again He went out from the region of Tyre, and came through Sidon to the Sea of Galilee, within the region of Decapolis. 32 And they brought to Him one who was deaf and spoke with difficulty, and they entreated Him to lay His hand upon him. 33 And He took him aside from the multitude by himself, and put His fingers into his ears, and after spitting, He touched his tongue with the saliva; 34 and looking up to heaven with a deep sigh, He said to him, "Ephphatha!" that is, "Be opened!" 35 And his ears were opened, and the impediment of his tongue was removed, and he began speaking plainly. 36 And He gave them orders not to tell anyone; but the more He ordered them, the more widely they continued to proclaim it. 37 And they were utterly astonished, saying, "He has done all things well; He makes even the deaf to hear, and the dumb to speak."

Mark 7:24-30

Testing a gentile woman's faith

Jesus now goes into non-Jewish territory. He ministers to Jews first, but He comes to save Gentiles also. Here, He first addresses a Syrophoenician woman whose little daughter is possessed by an unclean spirit. The woman keeps *asking Him to cast the demon out of her daughter.* Jesus' seemingly hard and insensitive reply is to test the reality of her faith in Him. Referring to Jews as *children* and Gentiles as *dogs*, He says the children must be fed first. Their food is not for dogs. He thereby demonstrates that His priority is sharing His message with Jews before approaching Gentiles. Her reply shows real faith in Him: *Yes, Lord, but even the dogs under the table feed on the children's crumbs.* Although Jesus must reach Jews first with His teaching and miraculous works, why cannot some Gentiles trust in Him too? Jesus says her answer, demonstrating her faith, causes her daughter's deliverance from her possessing demon. She goes home and finds this is true. Jesus' words always are true!

If Jesus does not save Gentiles, I could not tell you about Him now! With all non-Jews I would be eternally lost. But Jesus cares for all sorts of social 'outsiders'—including destitute, immoral or imprisoned people. He died on the cross for the 'world'[123]—for sinners of all types. He saves all who come to Him—whoever they are![124]

Mark 7:31-37

This deaf man who can hardly speak hears and speaks!

Decapolis is a stronghold of Gentile life, east of Jordan River. Its ten cities deeply reflect Greek culture. Jesus now visits Decapolis. A deaf man, able to speak only *with difficulty* is brought to Jesus, who is asked to lay hands on him. Jesus takes him aside, puts His fingers in his ears, and places His saliva on the mute man's tongue. The Son of God looks to Heaven, sighs deeply, and commands, *'Ephphatha!' that is, 'Be opened!'* The man hears and speaks plainly. Although Jesus tells people to say nothing, they publicise what Christ has done for him. (The reverse is, sadly, often

123. John 3:16.
124. Hebrews 7:25.

true today. The Bible says Christians should tell people about the Saviour. Sadly, we often fail to do so!) The astonished people remark, that Jesus *'has done all things well; He makes even the deaf to hear and the mute to speak.'*

Conversion to Christ is like this man's coming to hear and speak. Before becoming *born again*[125], non-Christians rarely sense God's speaking to them. The Bible's message is sealed until God's Holy Spirit opens spiritually deaf ears. Naturally we cannot understand God's word without the Holy Spirit.[126] With His help a new Christians starts understanding the Bible: there are no 'quick fixes'. His mouth is opened too! He begins to praise His Saviour God and share God's good news with others. His words will now comfort others, including new Christian brothers and sisters.

Questions on Chapter 27
Mark 7:24–37 Dealing with outsiders.

A. **Why does Jesus seem to speak negatively to the Syrophoenician woman? How does she respond? Do you think that Jesus is taken by surprise?** *Mark 7:26   Mark7:24-30   Luke 18:1-7   John 2:25*

B. **How does the miracle of healing on the deaf and partially mute man illustrate how God works in *spiritually* deaf and mute people?** *Mark 7:32-37* *Mark 8:18   Isaiah 29:18-19   Luke 7:22   Revelation 3:20   Hebrews 5:11   Hebrews 4:7*

C. **Do you agree that Jesus *has done all things well*? What things do you think that Jesus has done especially well in history and for you?** *Mark 7:37* *Genesis 1:31   John 3:17   Romans 5:9   Romans 8:37   Ephesians 2:18   1 John 4:9*

---

125. See John 3:3-7.
126. 1 Corinthians 2:14.

Chapter 28
Bread and blindness

Mark 8:1-26 (NASB)
[1] In those days again, when there was a great multitude and they had nothing to eat, He called His disciples and said to them, [2] "I feel compassion for the multitude because they have remained with Me now three days, and have nothing to eat; [3] and if I send them away hungry to their home, they will faint on the way; and some of them have come from a distance." [4] And His disciples answered Him, "Where will anyone be able to find enough to satisfy these men with bread here in a desolate place?" [5] And He was asking them, "How many loaves do you have?" And they said, "Seven." [6] And He directed the multitude to sit down on the ground; and taking the seven loaves, He gave thanks and broke them, and started giving them to His disciples to serve to them, and they served them to the multitude. [7] They also had a few small fish; and after He had blessed them, He ordered these to be served as well. [8] And they ate and were satisfied; and they picked up seven large baskets full of what was left over of the broken pieces. [9] And about four thousand were there; and He sent them away.

[10] And immediately He entered the boat with His disciples, and came to the district of Dalmanutha. [11] And the Pharisees came out and began to argue with Him, seeking from Him a sign from heaven, to test Him. [12] And sighing deeply in His spirit, He said, "Why does this generation seek for a sign? Truly I say to you, no sign shall be given to this generation." [13] And leaving them, He again embarked and went away to the other side. [14] And they had forgotten to take bread; and did not have more than one loaf in the boat with them. [15] And He was giving orders to them, saying, "Watch out! Beware of the leaven of the Pharisees and the leaven of Herod." [16] And they began to discuss with one another the fact that they had no bread. [17] And Jesus, aware of this, said to them, "Why do you discuss the fact that you have no bread? Do you not yet see

or understand? Do you have a hardened heart? [18] "HAVING EYES, DO YOU NOT SEE? AND HAVING EARS, DO YOU NOT HEAR? And do you not remember, [19] when I broke the five loaves for the five thousand, how many baskets full of broken pieces you picked up?" They said to Him, "Twelve." [20] "And when I broke the seven for the four thousand, how many large baskets full of broken pieces did you pick up?" And they said to Him, "Seven." [21] And He was saying to them, "Do you not yet understand?"

[22] And they came to Bethsaida. And they brought a blind man to Him, and entreated Him to touch him. [23] And taking the blind man by the hand, He brought him out of the village; and after spitting on his eyes, and laying His hands upon him, He asked him, "Do you see anything?" [24] And he looked up and said, "I see men, for I am seeing them like trees, walking about." [25] Then again He laid His hands upon his eyes; and he looked intently and was restored, and began to see everything clearly. [26] And He sent him to his home, saying, "Do not even enter the village."

Mark 8:1-9
Feeding four thousand

Jesus performs a miracle similar to feeding of the crowd which included five thousand men.[127] Here, He feeds four thousand men, and again probably many women and children. After hearing Jesus teach, they are hungry and without food. Jesus feeds them from seven loaves and a few small fish. Seven large baskets of scraps are collected after all have eaten plenty. A little later Jesus refers to both incidents, confirming each occurred. Surely these two miracles would convince everyone that Jesus is the Son of God?

Mark 8:10-12
The blindness of the pharisees

However, not the biased Pharisees! As Jesus and His disciples take a boat for

---

127. Mark 6:41.

Dalmanutha, they argue with Him asking for a sign from Heaven! In opposing Him they are blinded by prejudice. Sin always blinds unrepentant sinners, even if they lead others.[128] Jesus sighs and refuses to give another sign. (In any case, they probably would reject it.) Today people still crave for signs and wonders although they don't need them. God's revealed word, the Bible, leads honest seekers to faith in Christ. God's written revelation is the strongest possible evidence of His existence.

Mark 8:13-21
The blindness of the disciples

Jesus leaves for the other side by boat. One loaf only is in the boat. The disciples mistakenly think He refers to lack of bread when He warns *Beware of the leaven of the Pharisees and of Herod.* But Jesus refers to their ungodly influence, proud opposition, and rejection of Him. He reminds them that making bread from nothing is easy for Him, as He cites His two recent miraculous feedings of large crowds. His disciples are still blind to His identity, deaf to His words, and lack understanding.

Jesus' disciples still must concentrate on His character and works. Knowing who Jesus is and what He has done leads to understanding His word and why some oppose it.

Mark 8:22-26
A blind man sees

People plead with Jesus to touch and heal a blind man at Bethsaida. Leading him away by the hand Jesus spits on and touches his eyes, asking, *Do you see anything?* He sees men *like trees, walking around.* Jesus touches his eyes again. His sight is perfectly restored. He is sent home and told not to enter the village. Christ's personal involvement with the man, both by word and by touch, feature in this unique two-stage miracle.

---

128. Matthew 15:14.

An old lady, blind from birth, became a Christian. Her eyes of spiritual understanding were opened. She rejoiced that she was Heaven-bound and that the first person she would ever see would be Jesus!

Through the gospel Jesus can open your eyes, too.[129] John Newton says in, 'Amazing Grace', 'I once was blind, but now I see.' Do you understand about Jesus through new eyes?

Questions on Chapter 28
Mark 8:1–26 Bread and blindness.

A. How do you know that this further account of feeding thousands of people with hardly any food is not a confused contradiction of the first account? *Mark 8:6-9 Mark 6:41 Mark 8:19-20 2 Timothy 2:15*

B. Compare the blindness of the Pharisees with the blindness of the disciples. *Mark 8:14-22 Mark 8:11-12, 15 Matthew 15:12-14 Revelation 3:18 1 John 2:8-11*

C. In what ways is the healing of this blind man similar to other miracles performed by Jesus? In what way is it different? *Mark 8:22-24 Mark 8:25*

---

129. Acts 26:18.

Chapter 29
Questions Jesus asks

Disc Track 2 – 13

Mark 8:27-38 (NASB)

27 And Jesus went out, along with His disciples, to the villages of Caesarea Philippi; and on the way He questioned His disciples, saying to them, "Who do people say that I am?" 28 And they told Him, saying, "John the Baptist; and others say Elijah; but others, one of the prophets." 29 And He continued by questioning them, "But who do you say that I am?" Peter answered and said to Him, "Thou art the Christ." 30 And He warned them to tell no one about Him. 31 And He began to teach them that the Son of Man must suffer many things and be rejected by the elders and the chief priests and the scribes, and be killed, and after three days rise again. 32 And He was stating the matter plainly. And Peter took Him aside and began to rebuke Him. 33 But turning around and seeing His disciples, He rebuked Peter, and said, "Get behind Me, Satan; for you are not setting your mind on God's interests, but man's." 34 And He summoned the multitude with His disciples, and said to them, "If anyone wishes to come after Me, let him deny himself, and take up his cross, and follow Me. 35 "For whoever wishes to save his life shall lose it; but whoever loses his life for My sake and the gospel's shall save it. 36 "For what does it profit a man to gain the whole world, and forfeit his soul? 37 "For what shall a man give in exchange for his soul? 38 "For whoever is ashamed of Me and My words in this adulterous and sinful generation, the Son of Man will also be ashamed of him when He comes in the glory of His Father with the holy angels."

Mark 8:27–33
Who is Jesus—and why has he come?

En route to Caeserea Phillippi, Jesus asks His disciples, *Who do people say that I am?* They reply either John the Baptist, or Elijah, or *one of the prophets.* Jesus then asks directly, *Who do **you** say that I am?* Everyone needs to answer that question. The right reply can lead to a changed eternity after death and a changed life now, because it shows why we can trust Jesus.

Peter's immediate answer, elsewhere confirmed by Jesus as correct, [130] is *You are the Christ.* Old Testament students knew Messiah would come as prophet, priest and king to deliver sinners from sin, not as a military warlord to end Roman slavery. Peter partially grasps this. Jesus forbids the disciples to publicise that *the Son of Man* (Jesus Himself) *must suffer many things and be rejected by the elders and the chief priests and the scribes, and be killed, and after three days rise again.* It is not the right time for Him to die, so He now reveals His coming death and resurrection only to His disciples. Peter's response to hearing this is as wrong now as His previous statement *You are the Christ* was right before. Jesus rebukes him: Satan is behind Peter's response. Peter looks only from man's point of view. He still has missed that Jesus has come to die. Peter's eyes of understanding are still closed. As the blind man needs to receive physical sight, Peter needs to be converted in order to 'see' the truth spiritually.

Jesus is a wonderful teacher who works amazing miracles. His wisdom and power are matched only by His love. But His purpose in coming to this world is to die on the cross for our sins.[131] The only way to be forgiven is to trust in His death for our sins. Jesus predicts his resurrection after dying on the cross, He will rise again. We now know He did that. Now, as the living Saviour, He enters the lives of all those coming to Him for forgiveness.

---

130. Matthew 16:16.
131. Mark 10:45.

Mark 8:34-38
The other cross

After speaking about His coming death, Jesus teaches that coming to Him means self-denial, taking up the cross and following Him. The right to live selfishly is 'crossed out' in following Jesus. That right goes if Jesus is your Lord. Sharing His good news becomes your priority. You could actually lose your life for Him—many Christians have done so. But the worst bargain is to lose your soul eternally. If you could gain everything in the world—all its splendour, wealth, status and power—and go to a lost eternity, you would be a tragic loser. Your eternal soul is so precious that Jesus died to save it—to lose it is foolish, tragic and irreversible.

Jesus continues His direct teaching. No one can doubt how serious this issue is. If you are ashamed of Him and His words, He will be ashamed of you when He comes again. He urges everyone to turn from unbelief and selfishness and yield to Him. He is God. What He says is always right! 'Just do it!'[132]

Questions on Chapter 29
Mark 8:27-38 Questions Jesus asks.

A. **What does Peter get right here? Why is that important?** Mark 8:29 John 14:6
Acts 4:12 Matthew 1:21

B. **What does Peter get sadly wrong? Why is it important to get the issue of Jesus' death right?** Mark 8:31-33 Hebrews 9:22 Luke 19:10 1 Corinthians 15:3-4

C. **What does Jesus teach is the value of an eternal soul? Why does knowing that your soul is safe for eternity encourage you to deny yourself in order to follow Jesus?** Mark 8: 34-38 Luke 14:27

---

132. Heed the advice of His mother, Mary, in John 2:5.

Chapter 30
Jesus only

Mark 9:1-13 (ESV)
[1] And he said to them, "Truly, I say to you, there are some standing here who will not taste death until they see the kingdom of God after it has come with power." [2] And after six days Jesus took with him Peter and James and John, and led them up a high mountain by themselves. And he was transfigured before them, [3] and his clothes became radiant, intensely white, as no one on earth could bleach them. [4] And there appeared to them Elijah with Moses, and they were talking with Jesus. [5] And Peter said to Jesus, "Rabbi, it is good that we are here. Let us make three tents, one for you and one for Moses and one for Elijah." [6] For he did not know what to say, for they were terrified. [7] And a cloud overshadowed them, and a voice came out of the cloud, "This is my beloved Son; listen to him." [8] And suddenly, looking around, they no longer saw anyone with them but Jesus only. [9] And as they were coming down the mountain, he charged them to tell no one what they had seen, until the Son of Man had risen from the dead. [10] So they kept the matter to themselves, questioning what this rising from the dead might mean. [11] And they asked him, "Why do the scribes say that first Elijah must come?" [12] And he said to them, "Elijah does come first to restore all things. And how is it written of the Son of Man that he should suffer many things and be treated with contempt? [13] But I tell you that Elijah has come, and they did to him whatever they pleased, as it is written of him."

Mark 9:1-3
A glimpse of Jesus in his kingdom

Jesus promises that some of His hearers *will not taste death until they see the kingdom of God after it has come with power.* After six days, a glorious preview of His kingdom occurs on a mountain to Peter, James and John. Jesus is transfigured before them. He takes on some of His kingdom glory. His dazzlingly radiant clothes are intensely and exceptionally white. Christ's transfiguration points to the greater glory of Heaven!

Mark 9:4-8
Elijah and Moses—but 'Jesus only'

With the transfigured Saviour appear Elijah and Moses, talking with Him. Elijah represents God's prophets and Moses God's law, previously revealed through him. Together they stand for the Old Testament, later called *the Law and the Prophets* [133]by Jesus. Peter impetuously suggests that they make three tents, one each for Jesus, Moses and Elijah. He probably blurts this out in his scared confusion. Jesus says nothing. From an overshadowing cloud God the Father declares: *This is my beloved Son, listen to Him.* His eternal Son is His last word. Only Jesus has His final authority, fulfilling all that Moses, Elijah, and other Old Testament writers wrote or predicted about Him. The disciples *no longer* see anyone else *but Jesus only.* God the Father has confirmed the truth He just communicated. Jesus alone remains as His eternal Son. The whole Bible points to Him. We must trust Him as our Saviour, follow Him as our Lord, and listen to His voice through the Holy Spirit, as we daily read the Bible and hear it explained through clear preaching and teaching.

---

133. Luke 16:16.

Mark 9:9–13
Warning and prophecy

They descend the mountain. Jesus forbids them to mention this transfiguration experience until after His resurrection. They obey but have no idea what Jesus means by His *rising from the dead*. They ask Jesus why the scribes say Elijah must come before Messiah suffers. Jesus assures them that the prophecy in no way changes the Messiah's predicted suffering and death. As Messiah, Jesus has repeated that prophecy about His rejection, suffering, death and resurrection.

Jesus then implies Elijah's predicted coming was fulfilled in John the Baptist. Although not Elijah himself, John came in what Luke's Gospel calls *the spirit and power of Elijah.*[134]

In prayer we should follow the disciples' good example of putting our questions to Jesus. He will answer us from the Bible. Those answers rarely come immediately. We need patience. Often it takes time to 'click'!

Questions on Chapter 30
Mark 9:1–13 Jesus only.

A. How does the transfiguration of Jesus on the mountain fulfil the prediction that some will not taste death until they see the kingdom of God coming with power? *Mark 9:1 Mark 9:2-3*

B. What do you learn from the fact that only Jesus remains after Elijah and Moses depart? What do Elijah and Moses represent? *Hebrews 1:1-2 2 Chronicles 21:12 Malachi 4:5 John 1:17 Hebrews 3:1-6 John 7:19 Acts 13:39 Romans 10:5*

C. What good example do the disciples give when they are confused about understanding what Jesus has said? *Mark 9:11 Acts 17:11 Matthew 7:7-8 James 1:5*

---

134. Luke 1:17.

Chapter 31
The prayer God always answers

Mark 9:14-29 (ESV)
[14] And when they came to the disciples, they saw a great crowd around them, and scribes arguing with them. [15] And immediately all the crowd, when they saw him, were greatly amazed and ran up to him and greeted him. [16] And he asked them, "What are you arguing about with them?" [17] And someone from the crowd answered him, "Teacher, I brought my son to you, for he has a spirit that makes him mute. [18] And whenever it seizes him, it throws him down, and he foams and grinds his teeth and becomes rigid. So I asked your disciples to cast it out, and they were not able." [19] And he answered them, "O faithless generation, how long am I to be with you? How long am I to bear with you? Bring him to me." [20] And they brought the boy to him. And when the spirit saw him, immediately it convulsed the boy, and he fell on the ground and rolled about, foaming at the mouth. [21] And Jesus asked his father, "How long has this been happening to him?" And he said, "From childhood. [22] And it has often cast him into fire and into water, to destroy him. But if you can do anything, have compassion on us and help us." [23] And Jesus said to him, "'If you can'! All things are possible for one who believes." [24] Immediately the father of the child cried out and said, "I believe; help my unbelief!" [25] And when Jesus saw that a crowd came running together, he rebuked the unclean spirit, saying to it, "You mute and deaf spirit, I command you, come out of him and never enter him again." [26] And after crying out and convulsing him terribly, it came out, and the boy was like a corpse, so that most of them said, "He is dead." [27] But Jesus took him by the hand and lifted him up, and he arose. [28] And when he had entered the house, his disciples asked him privately, "Why could we not cast it out?" [29] And he said to them, "This kind cannot be driven out by anything but prayer."

Mark 9:14-16
Down from the mountain

Jesus, Peter, James and John, having descended the mountain, see the other disciples surrounded by a crowd. The scribes are there. Often after a time of blessing—like Jesus' transfiguration—difficult problems arise, often connected with awkward people! The amazed crowd greets Jesus, who asks, *What are you arguing about with them?*

Mark 9:17-24
The big problem and the far bigger prayer

The father of a spirit-possessed mute boy answers. He describes how his son's demon possession produces serious convulsions. The unclean spirit causes him to fall, foam at the mouth, grind his teeth, and become rigid. His father says that Jesus' disciples cannot liberate his boy by expelling his evil spirit. Jesus says His disciples, (whom He empowered earlier to cast out unclean spirits [135]), lack faith. Jesus has the boy brought to Him. Again convulsed by the spirit, he falls down and rolls around, foaming at the mouth. Jesus hears he has suffered like this from childhood, having been thrown into both fire and water. His father pleads, *If You can do anything, have compassion on us and help us.* Jesus assures him that all is possible for anyone trusting Him personally. That is what 'believe' means.

The man's reply is a wonderful prayer, encouraging today any feeling their faith is inadequate. He cries from the heart: *I believe; help my unbelief.* He takes his unbelief to Jesus and asks Him to put it right. Jesus will always do that!

Mark 9:25-27
Jesus alone can save

Reversing the father's unbelief and answering his prayer, Jesus commands the

---
135. Mark 3:15.

unclean spirit to leave the boy and never return. The demon obeys, convulsing the boy. He is so motionless that onlookers say *He is dead.* They are wrong! As Jesus takes the boy's hand and lifts him up, he arises.

The boy's deliverance parallels our saving faith in Christ. We can neither control all our actions nor save ourselves from sin and eternal death. We live physically, but are dead in our sins[136]. We are dead toward God. Only Jesus can save us.[137] He touches us through His pardoning death and powerful resurrection life. Responding to faith in Him, He takes us personally *by the hand.* Jesus alone gives us eternal life. His strength and love begin to control and direct our lives, giving us purpose and peace.

Mark 9:28-29
A word to the disciples

Jesus says that to liberate a boy like the one He healed, they must pray. We too must cultivate a time of daily prayer and trust Him![138]

Questions on Chapter 31
Mark 9:14-29 The prayer God always answers.

A. After a time of blessing on the mountain what do the disciples encounter with Jesus? Should you expect Satan to attack after a time of blessing? Mark 9:14-18   Matthew 3:16-17   Matthew 4:1-11   2 Corinthians 12:7   Job 1:6-12

B. Although the way that Jesus heals the spirit-possessed mute boy is another historical fact, how does it also illustrate how God works in a sinner who turns to Christ as his Saviour? Matthew 11:28   Ephesians 2:1   Romans 8:2

C. If you are assaulted by unbelief and doubts, how should you deal with them? How should your prayers be affected? Mark 9:24   Romans 10:17   Acts 17:31

---

136. Ephesians 2:1-2 tells the Ephesian Christians *you were dead in the trespasses and sins in which you once walked* until Christ gave them eternal life.
137. Romans 5:6.
138. Philippians 4:6.

Chapter 32
Important teaching on important subjects

Mark 9:30-50 (ESV)

[30] They went on from there and passed through Galilee. And he did not want anyone to know, [31] for he was teaching his disciples, saying to them, "The Son of Man is going to be delivered into the hands of men, and they will kill him. And when he is killed, after three days he will rise." [32] But they did not understand the saying, and were afraid to ask him. [33] And they came to Capernaum. And when he was in the house he asked them, "What were you discussing on the way?" [34] But they kept silent, for on the way they had argued with one another about who was the greatest. [35] And he sat down and called the twelve. And he said to them, "If anyone would be first, he must be last of all and servant of all." [36] And he took a child and put him in the midst of them, and taking him in his arms, he said to them, [37] "Whoever receives one such child in my name receives me, and whoever receives me, receives not me but him who sent me." [38] John said to him, "Teacher, we saw someone casting out demons in your name, and we tried to stop him, because he was not following us." [39] But Jesus said, "Do not stop him, for no one who does a mighty work in my name will be able soon afterward to speak evil of me. [40] For the one who is not against us is for us. [41] For truly, I say to you, whoever gives you a cup of water to drink because you belong to Christ will by no means lose his reward. [42] "Whoever causes one of these little ones who believe in me to sin, it would be better for him if a great millstone were hung around his neck and he were thrown into the sea. [43] And if your hand causes you to sin, cut it off. It is better for you to enter life crippled than with two hands to go to hell, to the unquenchable fire. [45] And if your foot causes you to sin, cut it off. It is better for you to enter life lame than with two feet to be thrown into hell. [47] And if your eye causes you to sin, tear it out. It is better for you to enter the kingdom of God with one eye than with two eyes to be thrown into hell, [48] 'where

> their worm does not die and the fire is not quenched.' ⁴⁹ For everyone will be salted with fire. ⁵⁰ Salt is good, but if the salt has lost its saltiness, how will you make it salty again? Have salt in yourselves, and be at peace with one another."

Mark 9:30-32
Another reminder

Jesus again reminds His disciples of His forthcoming rejection, suffering, death and resurrection. He wants no one to know He is in Galilee. Still it is not time to 'go public', outside His disciples, about His death.

Mark 9:33-37
Who is the greatest?

Amazingly, while Jesus predicts His rejection and death, His disciples argue about who is the greatest. Jesus says that the greatest person humbly serves everyone else and illustrates this from a child's humility. Christian humility is childlike.

Mark 9:38-41
Appreciate the work of others

John says that the disciples tried to stop a man casting out demons in Jesus' name, *because he was not following us.* Jesus states they are wrong. He wants people to do mighty works for Him. Anyone doing this cannot speak evil of Him afterwards. Jesus even will reward anyone giving His followers a cup of water to drink. We also must prize and esteem other Christians' work as they trust His word, preach His gospel, and support His followers. If Jesus values them, so should we.

Mark 9:42–50[139]
Judgement

Perhaps Christ's next words result from His recent reference to a child. Jesus warns of the grave consequences of causing little ones believing in Him to sin. This has dual application. Beware of damaging a young child in **any** way. God will avenge that, unless genuine repentance produces forgiveness through trusting Christ. Beware also of causing a newly born again Christian to stumble. However old that person is a 'born again' child of God through personal faith in Jesus.[140]. Anyone causing such a person to stumble must answer to God one day.

Jesus, expanding the thought of judgement, teaches it is better to lose your hand, foot or eye, if they make you sin, than to suffer Hell's eternal judgement in continuous fire. Jesus speaks figuratively. He never intends self-harming. Rather, he recommends drastic action to cut out our sins in repentance and to trust Him. There is no other way to know His forgiveness and escape Hell. Like salt, which preserved meat from going bad, repentance and faith in Christ will purify us and guard from sin's spreading corruption.

Questions on Chapter 32
Mark 9:30–50 Important teaching on important subjects.

A. Why does Jesus often remind the disciples that He must suffer, die and rise again? Why are His death and resurrection so very important? Mark 9:30-32 Acts 26:22-23 Luke 24:45-47 John 11:49-53 Acts 4:12

B. Why are the disciples shamed into silence at Jesus' question? What personal ambition should a Christian have? Mark 9:33-34 Philippians 3:7-10 Matthew 6:33   Matthew 16:24 Philippians 2:3

C. Consider God's hatred for sin. How will he judge those who sinfully cause His children to suffer? What do the severe illustrations of avoiding sinning teach about how to follow Christ? Mark 9:42 Mark 9:43-47 Romans 1:18 Romans 12:1-2 Luke 9:23

---

139.   Unlike NKJV (which follows AV and the 'Received Text'), ESV and NASB leave out verses 44 and 46. NIV includes them with a footnote. No truths here are changed by their omission, although they do emphasise the truths taught in the passage.
140.   John 3:16-18, John 3:36.

Chapter 33
How about divorce?

Mark 10:1-12 (ESV)
1 And he left there and went to the region of Judea and beyond the Jordan, and crowds gathered to him again. And again, as was his custom, he taught them. 2 And Pharisees came up and in order to test him asked, "Is it lawful for a man to divorce his wife?" 3 He answered them, "What did Moses command you?" 4 They said, "Moses allowed a man to write a certificate of divorce and to send her away." 5 And Jesus said to them, "Because of your hardness of heart he wrote you this commandment. 6 But from the beginning of creation, 'God made them male and female.' 7 'Therefore a man shall leave his father and mother and hold fast to his wife, 8 and the two shall become one flesh.' So they are no longer two but one flesh. 9 What therefore God has joined together, let not man separate." 10 And in the house the disciples asked him again about this matter. 11 And he said to them, "Whoever divorces his wife and marries another commits adultery against her, 12 and if she divorces her husband and marries another, she commits adultery."

Mark 10:1-2
A catch question

Jesus teaches in the region around Jordan. The Pharisees' testing question about divorce is: *Is it lawful for a man to divorce his wife?* However He answers, they seek to trap him.

Mark 10:3-9
A careful answer

Jesus hits the ball back into the Pharisees' court. He asks what Moses commanded in the law. They reply he *allowed a man to write a certificate of divorce and to send her away.* Jesus answers that hard human hearts caused Moses to allow this. From Scripture, Jesus shows God made humans *male and female*[141] from creation. God's will and plan is always for the man and woman who marry to be regarded as one. A man must leave his parents *and hold fast to his wife.* He should 'leave and cleave'. Thus Jesus reveals God's description of marriage as a union between one man and one woman for life. He emphasises this principle with, *What therefore God has joined together, let not man separate.*

Mark 10:10-12
Further explanation about divorce to his disciples

Briefly answering a question set to trap Him, Jesus avoids complicated messy divorce situations abounding even in His day, as today. The Bible gives guidance on those issues elsewhere.[142] Remember too that Christ's offer of forgiveness and restoration extends to all whose sins have smashed or spoiled marriages—whether theirs or others'.

Now Jesus answers the disciples about why God wants lasting marriages, not divorce: someone divorcing his or her spouse, and marrying another, commits adultery. The Bible is a single, unified book: this short passage must be read and blended with other Bible passages. Particularly relevant is Matthew 5:31-32, which carries Jesus' expansion of this basic teaching. Verse 32 says *But I say to you that everyone who divorces his wife, **except on the ground of sexual immorality**[143], makes her commit adultery, and whoever marries a divorced woman* [obviously in the circumstances Jesus covers here] *commits adultery.* Jesus never **commands** divorce where there

---

141. See Genesis 1:27; Genesis 5:2.
142. 1 Corinthians 7 deals with many different and complicated issues which are still with us in principle today.
143. My emphasis.

is adultery. Neither does He **commend** divorce for adultery. A marriage can survive despite the unfaithfulness of one or both spouses. Applying Moses' principle, Jesus confirms divorce is **allowed** where sexual immorality breaks a marriage. Even so, both parties should fight hard to try to save the marriage. The Bible clearly states that God hates divorce.[144] Divorce is only a tragic last resort when all else fails.

Questions on Chapter 33
Mark 10:1-12 How about divorce?

A. **What is God's best plan for marriage? Does the Bible anywhere teach that it is right for a man and a woman to live together and have sexual relationships outside marriage?** *Mark 10:6-9 1 Corinthians 6:18 Exodus 20:14 Mark 10:19 Colossians 3:5 Ephesians 5:3 Galatians 5:19 2 Corinthians 12:21*

B. **According to Jesus' teaching in verses 11 and 12, what ground for divorce is there, only if really necessary? How does this fit in with the context of Scripture as show by Matthew 5:31-32?** *Mark 10:11-12 Matthew 5:31-32*

C. **Why should a Christian strive to save his or her marriage, if at all possible?** *Mark 10:6-9 1 Peter 3:1-2 1 Peter 3:7*

---

144. Malachi 2:16 – This is very clear in other versions (e.g. in NIV, NASB and NKJV) and in the footnote of ESV. The primary ESV translation seems rather odd and at odds with the other versions.

A clear contrast—children and the rich young man

Disc Track
3 — 05

Mark 10:13-31 (ESV)
[13] And they were bringing children to him that he might touch them, and the disciples rebuked them. [14] But when Jesus saw it, he was indignant and said to them, "Let the children come to me; do not hinder them, for to such belongs the kingdom of God. [15] Truly, I say to you, whoever does not receive the kingdom of God like a child shall not enter it." [16] And he took them in his arms and blessed them, laying his hands on them. [17] And as he was setting out on his journey, a man ran up and knelt before him and asked him, "Good Teacher, what must I do to inherit eternal life?" [18] And Jesus said to him, "Why do you call me good? No one is good except God alone. [19] You know the commandments: 'Do not murder, Do not commit adultery, Do not steal, Do not bear false witness, Do not defraud, Honor your father and mother.'" [20] And he said to him, "Teacher, all these I have kept from my youth." [21] And Jesus, looking at him, loved him, and said to him, "You lack one thing: go, sell all that you have and give to the poor, and you will have treasure in heaven; and come, follow me." [22] Disheartened by the saying, he went away sorrowful, for he had great possessions. [23] And Jesus looked around and said to his disciples, "How difficult it will be for those who have wealth to enter the kingdom of God!" [24] And the disciples were amazed at his words. But Jesus said to them again, "Children, how difficult it is to enter the kingdom of God! [25] It is easier for a camel to go through the eye of a needle than for a rich person to enter the kingdom of God." [26] And they were exceedingly astonished, and said to him, "Then who can be saved?" [27] Jesus looked at them and said, "With man it is impossible, but not with God. For all things are possible with God." [28] Peter began to say to him, "See, we have left everything and followed you." [29] Jesus said, "Truly, I say to you, there is no one who has left house or brothers or sisters or mother or father or children or lands, for my sake and for the gospel, [30] who will not receive a hundredfold now in this time, houses and brothers and sisters and mothers and children and lands, with persecutions, and in the age to come eternal life. [31] But many who are first will be last, and the last first."

Mark 10:13-16
Faith like a child

Being annoyed with someone is not necessarily a sin if the anger is fair and controlled.[145] Sometimes we should be annoyed or angry over certain wrongs. Here, the disciples annoy Jesus. They rebuke people bringing children to Jesus. Jesus insists that children can come to Him unhindered. The kingdom of God is theirs. Before blessing them He states, *Truly, I say to you, whoever does not receive the kingdom of God like a child shall not enter it.* So Jesus confirms that some will be excluded from Heaven by their sins, and some will be accepted through personal saving faith in Christ alone. **How can you** *receive the kingdom of God like a child and so enter it?*

As a doting grandfather of six lovely little girls, I have rediscovered much about how children exercise trust! As I entered a hall with a hard polished wood floor one granddaughter stood on a table. With a big smile, she yelled out my name as she saw me. As I approached her, she spontaneously launched herself off the table towards me! She knew I would catch her—and she was right. I love her!

A guilty sinner must trust Jesus Christ *like a child*. Recognising his sin and guilt and that he deserves God's punishment, he casts himself on Jesus, who died on the cross in his place, loves him and is alive today. As he throws himself unconditionally into Christ's merciful arms, he is securely held. Jesus never drops anyone casting himself, on Him for cleansing and mercy. Just like my granddaughter trusted me, come and trust the Saviour. He will catch you! You *receive the kingdom* when He receives you in His arms!

Mark 10:17-31
The poor rich man

Matthew tells us that a certain rich man is young.[146] With many acquired riches, he expects a long luxurious life. But he is bankrupt spiritually. He runs and kneels before Jesus. He asks how he can *inherit eternal life*. He calls Jesus *'Good Teacher'*.

---

145. Ephesians 4:26, for example. Even righteous anger must be controlled by the one who is righteously angry.
146. Matthew 19:20.

Jesus underlines His deity by replying that only God is good. Jesus tells him to keep God's commandments, detailing the last six of the Ten Commandments,[147] except number ten, *You shall not covet*. The man says he has kept them all, so Jesus tests him. He tells him to sell everything and give it to the poor. He will then have treasure in Heaven. He calls him to follow Him. The man leaves, saddened. He does covet possessions. How long will his wealth last until he leaves it to enter a lost eternity? By putting his possessions before obeying God, he has also broken the first two commandments: he doesn't love God, and his possessions are his idols. How different from Christ who left Heaven's glories to empty Himself and die for us on the cross.[148]

Jesus teaches it is extremely hard—though not impossible, by God's grace—for a rich man to enter God's kingdom. It will take a miracle of grace. But receiving eternal life in Christ always needs God's miraculous grace!

The disciples say they have left everything to follow Christ. Jesus confirms they will gain, not only as possessors of eternal life, but because God compensates His followers generously in this life too. But *many who are first will be last, and the last first*. Better having little now, but to know God and His blessings eternally!

Questions on Chapter 34

Mark 10:13–31 A clear contrast—children and the rich young man.

A. **How is childlikeness a good example of how to put your trust in Jesus Christ?** Mark 10:14-15 Matthew 18:1-4

B. **How does Jesus get to the real heart of the problem of the poor rich man?** Mark 10:21 Mark 10:23-25 Exodus 20:17 Luke 12:15-21

C. **Did the man claim more about his righteousness and relationship with God than he actually experienced in practice? How can we deal with that temptation?** Mark 10:20 Psalm 51:6 Matthew 6:33 Colossians 3:2

---

147. See Exodus 20:12-17 and Deuteronomy 5:16-21. Note that in Mark 10:19 Jesus adds *Do not defraud* which is not in the Ten Commandments but is an application of three of them – no stealing, no false witness, and no coveting. Could it be that gaining wealth by fraud was part of the young man's problem?
148. Philippians 2:5-11; 2 Corinthians 8:9.

Chapter 35
Reminded, rebuked and restored

Disc 3 – Track 06

Mark 10:32-52 (ESV)
³² And they were on the road, going up to Jerusalem, and Jesus was walking ahead of them. And they were amazed, and those who followed were afraid. And taking the twelve again, he began to tell them what was to happen to him, ³³ saying, "See, we are going up to Jerusalem, and the Son of Man will be delivered over to the chief priests and the scribes, and they will condemn him to death and deliver him over to the Gentiles. ³⁴ And they will mock him and spit on him, and flog him and kill him. And after three days he will rise." ³⁵ And James and John, the sons of Zebedee, came up to him and said to him, "Teacher, we want you to do for us whatever we ask of you." ³⁶ And he said to them, "What do you want me to do for you?" ³⁷ And they said to him, "Grant us to sit, one at your right hand and one at your left, in your glory." ³⁸ Jesus said to them, "You do not know what you are asking. Are you able to drink the cup that I drink, or to be baptized with the baptism with which I am baptized?" ³⁹ And they said to him, "We are able." And Jesus said to them, "The cup that I drink you will drink, and with the baptism with which I am baptized, you will be baptized, ⁴⁰ but to sit at my right hand or at my left is not mine to grant, but it is for those for whom it has been prepared." ⁴¹ And when the ten heard it, they began to be indignant at James and John. ⁴² And Jesus called them to him and said to them, "You know that those who are considered rulers of the Gentiles lord it over them, and their great ones exercise authority over them. ⁴³ But it shall not be so among you. But whoever would be great among you must be your servant, ⁴⁴ and whoever would be first among you must be slave of all. ⁴⁵ For even the Son of Man came not to be served but to serve, and to give his life as a ransom for many." ⁴⁶ And they came to Jericho. And as he was leaving Jericho with his disciples and a great crowd, Bartimaeus, a blind beggar, the son of Timaeus, was sitting by the roadside. ⁴⁷ And when he heard that it was Jesus of Nazareth, he began to cry out and say, "Jesus, Son of David, have mercy on me!" ⁴⁸ And many rebuked him, telling him to be silent. But he cried out all the more, "Son of David,

have mercy on me!" [49] And Jesus stopped and said, "Call him." And they called the blind man, saying to him, "Take heart. Get up; he is calling you." [50] And throwing off his cloak, he sprang up and came to Jesus. [51] And Jesus said to him, "What do you want me to do for you?" And the blind man said to him, "Rabbi, let me recover my sight." [52] And Jesus said to him, "Go your way; your faith has made you well." And immediately he recovered his sight and followed him on the way.

Mark 10:32–34

The disciples are reminded again

Jesus reminds His disciples in greater detail about His coming rejection, suffering, and death. His trial and resultant death sentence will be unconstitutional and unlawful. He will be falsely accused of having broken Jewish law. He will be executed for His alleged offence of blasphemy under Roman law although He has not broken Roman law either!

Jesus makes this striking prediction of His wicked mistreatment and death, on His way to Jerusalem.

Mark 10:35–45

James and John

Zebedee's sons, James and John, ask Jesus to give them what they ask. They want to sit at His right and left hands in glory. Jesus says they don't know what they ask. Jesus must drain the cup of suffering—His death on the cross—before resuming His rightful place on Heaven's throne. He predicts their suffering, but is not allocating places in Heaven. They are already prepared. The other ten disciples resent the two brothers' selfish requests. Jesus reminds them all that a true servant qualifying for such 'promotion' does not promote himself. The greatest person in glory will serve others humbly as a slave now. He adds: *For even the Son of Man came not to be served but to serve, and to give His life as a ransom for many.* Jesus is the universe's greatest Person, but He will plumb the depths of servanthood,[149] even to die on a cross for us. Only His loving and gracious humility will enable Him to die, and to *give His life as a ransom for many.*

149. Philippians 2:6-8 especially verse 7.

Mark 10:46-52
Blind Bartimaeus

Jesus gives sight to a blind man, Bartimaeus, in Jericho. This factual, historic event again pictures a sinner turning from spiritual blindness that darkens his or her understanding. How this blind man comes to see, know and follow Jesus is repeated spiritually whenever Jesus saves a guilty sinner. This helpless beggar can do nothing to save himself from sin's penalty but cries out to Jesus for mercy. That is exactly how we come to Christ. Jesus willingly shows mercy to all who are sorry for their sins and call on Him to forgive and change them.[150] Bartimaeus calls Jesus *Son of David*, addressing Him as the Messiah coming to save. Jesus stops and tells the people to call the blind man. They do so, telling him to *Take heart*. They know how Jesus can change people! Throwing off his coat and springing to Jesus, he asks, *Rabbi, let me recover my sight.* He knows his need and shares it with Jesus. That is still how people come to Him today. Jesus responds immediately: *Go your way; your faith has made you well.* Jesus forgives immediately those who come to Him sincerely. No one needs to ask Jesus twice for mercy to be saved! Bartimaeus sees again and follows Jesus. All receiving Christ's new life have their eyes opened. Now they 'see' who Jesus really is. They start understanding biblical truth and follow Jesus. Is that your experience too?

Questions on Chapter 35
Mark 10:32-52 Reminded, rebuked and restored.

A. Here again, Jesus reminds His disciples about His coming rejection, suffering and death? Why do you think He reminds them of this so soon after the last warning? Mark 10:32-34 1 Timothy 4:6 1 Corinthians 11:24-25 Exodus 20:8 John 16:4

B. What are the two main reasons stated why Jesus came? How does His example compare with some rulers? Mark 10:45 Mark 10:42-44

C. Consider how Jesus deals with blind Bartimaeus. What lessons do you learn about helping those who 'cannot see' the truth of the gospel? Mark 10:46-52

---

150. Remember the humble publican whose cry for mercy was answered, whereas the religious Pharisee remained lost in his self-righteousness. Read Luke 18:9-14 especially verse 13.

Chapter 36
Jesus at Jerusalem

Mark 11:1-11 (ESV)
1 Now when they drew near to Jerusalem, to Bethphage and Bethany, at the Mount of Olives, Jesus sent two of his disciples 2 and said to them, "Go into the village in front of you, and immediately as you enter it you will find a colt tied, on which no one has ever sat. Untie it and bring it. 3 If anyone says to you, 'Why are you doing this?' say, 'The Lord has need of it and will send it back here immediately.'" 4 And they went away and found a colt tied at a door outside in the street, and they untied it. 5 And some of those standing there said to them, "What are you doing, untying the colt?" 6 And they told them what Jesus had said, and they let them go. 7 And they brought the colt to Jesus and threw their cloaks on it, and he sat on it. 8 And many spread their cloaks on the road, and others spread leafy branches that they had cut from the fields. 9 And those who went before and those who followed were shouting, "Hosanna! Blessed is he who comes in the name of the Lord! 10 Blessed is the coming kingdom of our father David! Hosanna in the highest!" 11 And he entered Jerusalem and went into the temple. And when he had looked around at everything, as it was already late, he went out to Bethany with the twelve.

Mark 11:1–7
Preparation to enter Jerusalem

Jesus nears Jerusalem with His disciples. At Bethpage and Bethany, close to the Mount of Olives, He sends two to a nearby village to find and fetch a tethered colt. The colt has never been ridden. When challenged they reply as Jesus instructed, *The Lord has need of it and will send it back here, immediately.* They are allowed to leave with the colt. They bring it to Jesus and throw their clothes on it. Jesus, the

Master of creation, sits on the unbroken colt.

Mark 11:8-10
An enthusiastic reception

He rides the colt towards Jerusalem. Although Jesus came to be the Saviour from sin, the crowds expect a political or military leader to deliver them from Roman domination. Although His fame has spread, understanding is lacking of who He is and of His real mission to come to die to save sinners. Clothes and leafy branches are spread before Him, signifying submission to Him, their hoped for political deliverer. They cry out *Hosanna! Blessed is He who comes in the name of the Lord! Blessed is the coming kingdom of our father David! Hosanna in the highest!*

Ironically the crowds cry, '*Hosanna*', means 'save now'. Jesus *has come to seek and to save the lost,*[151] but not militarily. How sad that they are not asking to be saved from their sins and from Hell's deserved eternal punishment. Jesus will soon hang nailed to a cross, punished as sin-bearer and substitute, but that is nowhere in their thinking. They are completely unaware that He will rise from the dead, and will 'save now' anyone repenting and coming to Him. Their ignorant shouts of *Hosanna!* are superficial and temporary. Soon Jesus will die in Jerusalem, to where He now travels. The enthusiastic cries of *Hosanna!* will then turn to cruel and crude baying for His blood, as the snarling cry of the angry mob will become *Crucify Him!*[152]

Mark 11:11
Jesus enters Jerusalem and surveys the temple

Jesus enters Jerusalem. He goes into the temple, God's house. He surveys everything in it. Soon, He will return to purify it by ejecting those who are misusing it. He now looks around to see for Himself what has been happening. How wise to check the situation personally before acting! Doubtless the temple also reminds Jesus of the holiness and splendour of His Father God and how He should be approached and worshipped.

---

151. Luke 19:10.
152. Mark 15:13-14.

It is now late. He returns with His disciples to Bethany. Jerusalem will see Him again, to live His last days on earth.

The first ten chapters of Mark's Gospel cover three years of Jesus' life. The last six chapters focus on His last eight crucial days. They cover His rejection, crucifixion and resurrection, and how they affect those trusting Him.

Questions on Chapter 36
Mark 11:1-11 Jesus at Jerusalem.

A. What do you notice about the sovereignty of our Lord Jesus Christ? What shows He is in control? Mark 11:1-6

B. 'Hosanna' means 'save now'? What do you think the crowd means by that? Why did they later cry 'Crucify Him'? Mark 11:9-10 Mark 15:13-14 1 Peter 3:18

C. What does Jesus do when He goes to the temple? How important is it to be properly informed before you act on an important issue? Mark 11:11 Mark 11:15-19

Chapter 37
Straight talk

Mark 11:12-33 (ESV)

¹² On the following day, when they came from Bethany, he was hungry. ¹³ And seeing in the distance a fig tree in leaf, he went to see if he could find anything on it. When he came to it, he found nothing but leaves, for it was not the season for figs. ¹⁴ And he said to it, "May no one ever eat fruit from you again." And his disciples heard it. ¹⁵ And they came to Jerusalem. And he entered the temple and began to drive out those who sold and those who bought in the temple, and he overturned the tables of the money-changers and the seats of those who sold pigeons. ¹⁶ And he would not allow anyone to carry anything through the temple. ¹⁷ And he was teaching them and saying to them, "Is it not written, 'My house shall be called a house of prayer for all the nations'? But you have made it a den of robbers." ¹⁸ And the chief priests and the scribes heard it and were seeking a way to destroy him, for they feared him, because all the crowd was astonished at his teaching. ¹⁹ And when evening came they went out of the city. ²⁰ As they passed by in the morning, they saw the fig tree withered away to its roots. ²¹ And Peter remembered and said to him, "Rabbi, look! The fig tree that you cursed has withered." ²² And Jesus answered them, "Have faith in God. ²³ Truly, I say to you, whoever says to this mountain, 'Be taken up and thrown into the sea,' and does not doubt in his heart, but believes that what he says will come to pass, it will be done for him. ²⁴ Therefore I tell you, whatever you ask in prayer, believe that you have received it, and it will be yours. ²⁵ And whenever you stand praying, forgive, if you have anything against anyone, so that your Father also who is in heaven may forgive you your trespasses." ²⁶ [But if you do not forgive, neither will your Father who is in heaven forgive your trespasses.] ²⁷ And they came again to Jerusalem. And as he was walking in the temple, the chief priests and the scribes and the elders came to him, ²⁸ and they said to him,

> "By what authority are you doing these things, or who gave you this authority to do them?" [29] Jesus said to them, "I will ask you one question; answer me, and I will tell you by what authority I do these things. [30] Was the baptism of John from heaven or from man? Answer me." [31] And they discussed it with one another, saying, "If we say, 'From heaven,' he will say, 'Why then did you not believe him?' [32] But shall we say, 'From man'?"--they were afraid of the people, for they all held that John really was a prophet. [33] So they answered Jesus, "We do not know." And Jesus said to them, "Neither will I tell you by what authority I do these things."

Mark 11:12-14
The fruitless fig tree

Travelling back to Jerusalem from Bethany the next day, Jesus is hungry. A fig tree in leaf is figless. Jesus curses it[153] by saying *May no one ever eat fruit from you again*. Palestinian fig trees bear early crops of immature fruit, appearing before the leaves, which provide food for the peasants. This tree is barren. The fig tree also symbolises Israel, God's chosen people, who also are fruitless. Perhaps Jesus indicates God's displeasure with them by cursing the tree?

Mark 11:15-18
Putting the temple right

Jesus activates His plan to purify the temple. Commercial transactions, selling pigeons for sacrifice, money changing, and dishonest dealings replace worship and prayer there. Like the fig tree and Israel, it is also fruitless. Jesus drives out the buyers and sellers, overturns the tables of the money changers, and upends the pigeon sellers' seats. He complains, *Is it not written, 'My house shall be called a house of prayer for all the nations'? But you have made it a den of robbers*. He forbids the use of the temple as a shortcut for commercial traffic, knowing that purifying it will incur

---

153. Jesus' curse of the fig tree is not bad language or temper. It is His expression of judgement to come.

the Jewish religious leaders' opposition. They want Him dead. Because His teaching astonishes the crowd they fear Him even more. Christians also must sometimes publicly stand for what is right, thereby facing unpopularity and opposition.

The Bible teaches that born again Christians' bodies[154] are temples of the Holy Spirit, as God resides within. Every real Christian is bought by Christ's blood and indwelt by God's Spirit. This temple passage reminds Christians to honour God with the way they keep and use the 'temples' of their bodies.[155]

Mark 11:19–26
Back to the fig tree

Jesus and His disciples leave Jerusalem that evening. Returning the next morning, they see that the cursed fig tree withered already. Peter tells Jesus, who immediately teaches the disciples that God can do the impossible. They must trust Him when praying. God answers prayer and moves mountains in their lives. Jesus emphasises the need to forgive anyone who has wronged them, before starting to pray. Their prayers can only be heard because God has forgiven their sins. We also must forgive others.

Mark 11:27–33
The authority of Jesus

Back in Jerusalem's temple the chief priests, scribes and elders ask Jesus where His authority comes from. If He says 'from God'[156] they will say He is blaspheming or mad. If He answers differently they will claim that He has no authority. Jesus' response turns the tables again! Was John the Baptist's authority God-given or man-made? Knowing people regarded John as God's prophet, they won't reply. Jesus too refuses to comment on His authority (which obviously is from God!)

---

154. In fact the only Christian known to the Bible is a 'born again Christian.' With out being born again, like Nicodemus we can neither 'see' (= 'understand') nor 'enter' the 'kingdom of God.' Read John 3: 3 and 5.
155. 1 Corinthians 6:19-20. This is in the immediate context of rejecting sexual immorality but also covers a wider principle of holy living in which the body is used to glorify God.
156. The meaning here of 'from heaven'.

Questions on Chapter 37
Mark 11:12–33 Straight talk.

A. From this passage what lessons can you learn from the fig tree and about Jesus? *Mark 11:12-14 Mark 11:19-26*

B. Why is Jesus so strongly opposed to the misuse and abuse of the temple? As the Christian's body is referred to as 'the temple of the Holy Spirit' in 1 Corinthians 6:19, how does the way Jesus regards the temple challenge Christians today? *Mark 11:15-18 1 Corinthians 6:19 Romans 12:1-2*

C. What can you learn from Jesus about how to answer a tricky question intended to trap you? *Mark 11:27-33 Mark 12:13-17*

Chapter 38
Setting traps for Jesus

3 – 09

Mark 12:1-27 (ESV)
[1] And he began to speak to them in parables. "A man planted a vineyard and put a fence around it and dug a pit for the winepress and built a tower, and leased it to tenants and went into another country. [2] When the season came, he sent a servant to the tenants to get from them some of the fruit of the vineyard. [3] And they took him and beat him and sent him away empty-handed. [4] Again he sent to them another servant, and they struck him on the head and treated him shamefully. [5] And he sent another, and him they killed. And so with many others: some they beat, and some they killed. [6] He had still one other, a beloved son. Finally he sent him to them, saying, 'They will respect my son.' [7] But those tenants said to one another, 'This is the heir. Come, let us kill him, and the inheritance will be ours.' [8] And they took him and killed him and threw him out of the vineyard. [9] What will the owner of the vineyard do? He will come and destroy the tenants and give the vineyard to others. [10] Have you not read this Scripture: "'The stone that the builders rejected has become the cornerstone; [11] this was the Lord's doing, and it is marvellous in our eyes'?" [12] And they were seeking to arrest him but feared the people, for they perceived that he had told the parable against them. So they left him and went away. [13] And they sent to him some of the Pharisees and some of the Herodians, to trap him in his talk. [14] And they came and said to him, "Teacher, we know that you are true and do not care about anyone's opinion. For you are not swayed by appearances, but truly teach the way of God. Is it lawful to pay taxes to Caesar, or not? Should we pay them, or should we not?" [15] But, knowing their hypocrisy, he said to them, "Why put me to the test? Bring me a denarius and let me look at it." [16] And they brought one. And he said to them, "Whose likeness and inscription is this?" They said to him, "Caesar's." [17] Jesus said to them, "Render to Caesar the things that are Caesar's, and to God the things that are

God's." And they marvelled at him. [18] And Sadducees came to him, who say that there is no resurrection. And they asked him a question, saying, [19] "Teacher, Moses wrote for us that if a man's brother dies and leaves a wife, but leaves no child, the man must take the widow and raise up offspring for his brother. [20] There were seven brothers; the first took a wife, and when he died left no offspring. [21] And the second took her, and died, leaving no offspring. And the third likewise. [22] And the seven left no offspring. Last of all the woman also died. [23] In the resurrection, when they rise again, whose wife will she be? For the seven had her as wife." [24] Jesus said to them, "Is this not the reason you are wrong, because you know neither the Scriptures nor the power of God? [25] For when they rise from the dead, they neither marry nor are given in marriage, but are like angels in heaven. [26] And as for the dead being raised, have you not read in the book of Moses, in the passage about the bush, how God spoke to him, saying, 'I am the God of Abraham, and the God of Isaac, and the God of Jacob'? [27] He is not God of the dead, but of the living. You are quite wrong."

Mark 12:1-12
A story which really stings

Avoiding forthright speech which could accelerate the religious leaders' attempts to kill Him, Jesus now speaks in parables. Meaning God the Father, He talks about a vineyard owner leasing his vineyard to tenants. The rent is proportional to the grapes harvested. The tenants, recognised by the Jewish leaders as themselves, won't pay their rent. The vineyard owner successively sends three servants, and then many others, to ask the tenants to pay their rent. Similarly, God sent His prophets to disobedient Israel to demand they abandon their rebellion and submit to God. As this parable shows, God's messengers were ignored, rejected, beaten, or even killed. Finally, in the parable, the owner sends his *beloved son*. Showing no respect for him, they kill him, reasoning that because he is dead no one will inherit the owner's vineyard. Jesus says the owner will come to destroy the tenants and give the vineyard to others.

Jesus is clearly predicting that the Jews will kill Him, God's eternal Son. He has come to die on the cross to save us. But God the Father's judgement will crush those guilty rebels who reject Christ. The parable also foresees blessing coming to others because of the Jews' rejection of Jesus—surely referring to Gentiles' coming to know Christ as Saviour and Lord.[157] Jesus then quotes from Psalm 118, [158] referring to Him as the rejected stone that becomes the cornerstone of the building. The religious leaders passionately want Jesus arrested but are scared of the people. They will seize Him later.

Mark 12:13-17
Dodging taxes?

The Herodians again combine with their sworn enemies, the Pharisees, in a cynical attempt to trap Jesus. If He can be made to speak against their Roman rulers, perhaps the Romans will arrest and kill Him for treason. They ask whether they, an occupied country, should pay Caesar taxes. Jesus asks whose features figure on the coins. They reply *Caesar's*. Christ's logical reply leaves them speechless: *Render to Caesar the things that are Caesar's, and to God the things that are God's.* That says all they need to know—and nothing that traps Him! What wisdom!

Mark 12:18-27
One wife for seven brothers!

Another Jewish religious group now seeks to discredit Jesus. The Sadducees, unlike the Pharisees, believe in neither the resurrection nor the miraculous. Hypothetically, they mention a woman who marries seven brothers in turn, after each previous brother dies. They ask whose wife she will be after she dies. Jesus shows their two-fold error, that they are ignorant both of God's power and of His Scriptures.

First, the Scriptures reveal marriage doesn't exist in Heaven. Sex is a God-given gift exclusively for marriage on earth, but no sexual distinction or activity occurs in Heaven. Heaven is perfect without it, in Christ's glorious presence.

---

157. Romans 11:1-27, especially verses 17-27.
158. Psalm 118:22-24.

Second, God says, *I* **am**[159] *the God of Abraham, and the God of Isaac, and the God of Jacob*—not I **was** their God. Although physically dead, they are clearly alive spiritually through the resurrection. God is the God of the living! The person who trusts Christ now immediately receives eternal life, a different spiritual life which is everlasting in length. Christians will enjoy it forever in God's new heaven and earth in perfect resurrection bodies that God will give to each Christian![160]

Questions on Chapter 38
Mark 12:1-27 Setting traps for Jesus.

A. How does the parable about the vineyard mirror the religious leaders' opposition to Jesus? *Mark 12:1-8   Mark 10:32-34   Matthew 23:28-32   Mark 15:15-25*

B. Consider the question in verses 13 and 14 put to trick Jesus. Why does his answer amaze them? *Mark 12:13-14   Mark 12:15-17   Romans 13: 1, 6-7*

C. What important truth do the Sadducees attack? What are their two big errors? To prove the resurrection how does Jesus blend Bible and logic? *Mark 12:18-23   Mark 12:24   Mark 12:25-27   Romans 8:34   2 Timothy 2:15   2 Timothy 3:16*

---

159. My emphasis.
160. 1 Corinthians 15:42-57, 1 Thessalonians 4:13-18.

Chapter 39
Sincerity, deity, hypocrisy, and generosity

Mark 12:28-44 (ESV)
28 And one of the scribes came up and heard them disputing with one another, and seeing that he answered them well, asked him, "Which commandment is the most important of all?" 29 Jesus answered, "The most important is, 'Hear, O Israel: The Lord our God, the Lord is one. 30 And you shall love the Lord your God with all your heart and with all your soul and with all your mind and with all your strength.' 31 The second is this: 'You shall love your neighbor as yourself.' There is no other commandment greater than these." 32 And the scribe said to him, "You are right, Teacher. You have truly said that he is one, and there is no other besides him. 33 And to love him with all the heart and with all the understanding and with all the strength, and to love one's neighbor as oneself, is much more than all whole burnt offerings and sacrifices." 34 And when Jesus saw that he answered wisely, he said to him, "You are not far from the kingdom of God." And after that no one dared to ask him any more questions. 35 And as Jesus taught in the temple, he said, "How can the scribes say that the Christ is the son of David? 36 David himself, in the Holy Spirit, declared, "'The Lord said to my Lord, Sit at my right hand, until I put your enemies under your feet.' 37 David himself calls him Lord. So how is he his son?" And the great throng heard him gladly. 38 And in his teaching he said, "Beware of the scribes, who like to walk around in long robes and like greetings in the marketplaces 39 and have the best seats in the synagogues and the places of honor at feasts, 40 who devour widows' houses and for a pretense make long prayers. They will receive the greater condemnation." 41 And he sat down opposite the treasury and watched the people putting money into the offering box. Many rich people put in large sums. 42 And a poor widow came and put in two small copper coins, which make a penny. 43 And he called his disciples to him and said to them, "Truly, I say to you, this poor widow has put in more than all those who are contributing to the offering box. 44 For they all contributed out of their abundance, but she out of her poverty has put in everything she had, all she had to live on."

Mark 12:28-34

The greatest—and the second greatest—commandments

Not all religious leaders are selfish and hypocritical in opposing God's truth. Like a breath of fresh air, we meet a scribe who is impressed by Jesus' answers to his colleagues. He asks Jesus, *Which commandment is the most important of all?* Jesus replies from Deuteronomy, something known by every serious Jew: *Hear, O Israel, the LORD our God, the LORD is one. And you shall love the LORD your God with all your heart, with all your soul, with all your mind, and with all your strength.*[161] This summarises the first four of the Ten Commandments, concerning our duty towards God.[162] Jesus volunteers the second commandment is like it, *You shall love your neighbour as yourself.* That summarises the last six of the Ten Commandments, showing how to treat others.[163]

The scribe applauds Christ's answer. He considers that loving God and others from the heart and with understanding dwarfs outward ceremonies, of offering sacrifices. He is not yet converted to Christ, but Jesus tells him, *You are not far from the kingdom of God.* Previously he probably wrongly considered himself in God's kingdom. Anyone aware that he must honour God completely, and treat others kindly and rightly, will recognise his own unworthiness and guilt. If that causes him to come to Christ, who shed His blood on the cross to pay the penalty for all repentant sinners, Jesus will enter, indwell and start to remake him through God's Holy Spirit,.

This man is **not far**[164] *from the kingdom of God.* But he is not there yet! He still needs to repent and trust Christ to get there. Are you far away, near, or there?

Mark 12:35-37

Jesus, the eternal Son of God, is Lord

Jesus teaches in the temple. Using David's Psalm 110: 1, He asks, *How can the scribes say that the Christ is the Son of David?* (that is, Messiah). David calls Him *Lord.* How can David's son also be David's eternal Lord? Jesus' question skilfully underlines that He, the Messiah, is both God and man. One hymn calls Him 'great

---

161. Deuteronomy 6:4-5. This is known as the 'Shema' by Jewish people.
162. Exodus 20:1-11; Deuteronomy 5:6-15.
163. Exodus 20:12-17; Deuteronomy 5:16-21.
164. My emphasis.

David's greater Son.'

The Deity of Christ is clearly taught in the Bible, but not always easy to grasp. Yet *the great throng* of ordinary people *heard Him gladly*. When the Holy Spirit works, Joe Public can receive and accept deep Bible truths, if faithfully held and simply explained.

Mark 12:38-44
Hypocrisy and generosity

Jesus criticises the scribes' hypocritical, self-seeking, showy falsehood. Whilst exploiting poor widows financially, they enjoy acclaim, greetings, and honour in high places at feasts. They will receive *greater condemnation* for that. They are religious, but lost.[165] All sinners need Christ—especially religious sinners.

Jesus watches people giving into the temple treasury. Many richer donors donate large amounts, some ostentatiously. A poor widow gives her two small copper coins—all that she has. Jesus tells His disciples that her sacrificial gift is *out of her poverty*. It is greater than others' 'larger' gifts. Christ loves sacrificial giving from the heart.

Questions on Chapter 39
Mark 12:28-44 Sincerity, deity, hypocrisy and generosity.

A. **How do the two commandments, regarded as the greatest by Jesus, summarise so well the Ten Commandments?** *Exodus 20:1-17 Mark 12:29-31 Mark 12:32-34 Romans 14:9*

B. **What does Jesus' logic in verses 35-37 teach you about who He really is?** *Mark 12:35-37 2 Peter 1:21 John 10:35*

C. **Why does Jesus regard the poor widow as the most generous person in the temple, and what challenging lesson does it put to Christians about giving to God's work?** *Mark 12:41-43 Mark 12:44 2 Corinthians 8:12*

---

165. Remember, for example Nicodemus in John 3 was a sincere man and a religious leader, but he was not yet saved before He came to Jesus, who made it quite clear that he needed to be 'born again'.

Chapter 40
The second coming of the Lord Jesus Christ (Part A)

Mark 13:1-23 (NKJV)
[1] Then as He went out of the temple, one of His disciples said to Him, "Teacher, see what manner of stones and what buildings are here!" [2] And Jesus answered and said to him, "Do you see these great buildings? Not one stone shall be left upon another, that shall not be thrown down." [3] Now as He sat on the Mount of Olives opposite the temple, Peter, James, John, and Andrew asked Him privately, [4] "Tell us, when will these things be? And what will be the sign when all these things will be fulfilled?"

[5] And Jesus, answering them, began to say: "Take heed that no one deceives you. [6] "For many will come in My name, saying, 'I am He,' and will deceive many. [7] "But when you hear of wars and rumors of wars, do not be troubled; for such things must happen, but the end is not yet. [8] "For nation will rise against nation, and kingdom against kingdom. And there will be earthquakes in various places, and there will be famines and troubles. These are the beginnings of sorrows. [9] "But watch out for yourselves, for they will deliver you up to councils, and you will be beaten in the synagogues. You will be brought before rulers and kings for My sake, for a testimony to them. [10] "And the gospel must first be preached to all the nations. [11] "But when they arrest you and deliver you up, do not worry beforehand, or premeditate what you will speak. But whatever is given you in that hour, speak that; for it is not you who speak, but the Holy Spirit. [12] "Now brother will betray brother to death, and a father his child; and children will rise up against parents and cause them to be put to death. [13] "And you will be hated by all for My name's sake. But he who endures to the end shall be saved.

[14] "So when you see the 'abomination of desolation,' spoken of by Daniel the prophet, standing where it ought not" (let the reader understand), "then let those who are in Judea flee to the mountains. [15] "Let him who is on the housetop not go down into the house, nor enter to take anything out of his house. [16] "And let him who is in the field not go back to get his clothes. [17] "But woe to those who are pregnant and to those

who are nursing babies in those days! [18] "And pray that your flight may not be in winter. [19] "For in those days there will be tribulation, such as has not been since the beginning of the creation which God created until this time, nor ever shall be. [20] "And unless the Lord had shortened those days, no flesh would be saved; but for the elect's sake, whom He chose, He shortened the days. [21] "Then if anyone says to you, 'Look, here is the Christ!' or, 'Look, He is there!' do not believe it. [22] "For false christs and false prophets will rise and show signs and wonders to deceive, if possible, even the elect. [23] "But take heed; see, I have told you all things beforehand.

Mark 13:1-4
The timetable

Jesus tells one disciple, awestruck by the temple building, that earthly things will pass away. Every temple stone will be thrown down. On the Mount of Olives, opposite the temple, Peter, James, John and Andrew ask Jesus about the timing of this, and the sign that it will happen. They want a miracle as an alarm.

Mark 13:5-23
The tribulation

Ignoring their specific questions, Jesus puts them on guard, He wants them to discern about the coming tribulation. He stresses that His gospel must be preached. He encourages their witness, forewarns about family division and betrayal, underlines God's sovereignty, and encourages perseverance.

Partial local fulfilment of prophecy has occurred already, such as Jerusalem's destruction and the temple's desecration. Greater global future fulfilment will follow. In fulfilling short term prophecies God assures us that long term prophecies will come to pass too.

Jesus warns about the intense period of tribulation, pressure and opposition. Even today, 200,000 Christians are estimated murdered or executed each year. The tribulation cauldron will increasingly bubble up in clusters until the whole troubled world boils furiously. The Christian church will be the main target. Despite this, eternal blessing awaits those trusting Christ to save them from sin's penalty and power.

Jesus states what is to come. Deceivers will come in His name. Increasingly, wars and rumours of wars, widespread earthquakes, and famines and troubles will signal the start of the sorrows. Christians will face serious, violent opposition from officialdom and organised religion. In all nations gospel preachers will be arrested, but God will enable them to testify.

In deteriorating family relationships, family members will betray each other to death. Christ's followers, hated for bearing His name, will endure to the end and be saved by God. The *abomination of desolation spoken of by Daniel*[166] probably prefigures Jerusalem's temple's desecration in AD 70. Jerusalem's fall foreshadows the final great trouble for God's people before Christ's return. The need to flee will be urgent. Jesus' said the huge turmoil will be *such as has not been since the beginning of creation which God created until this time, nor ever shall be*. False christs promoted by false prophets will use signs and wonders that even test God's elect.

But Christ will come again in power and glory to rule and to wrap up history![167] How vital and how wonderful to know Him as your Saviour and Lord now!

Questions on Chapter 40
Mark 13:1-23 The second coming of the Lord Jesus Christ (Part A).

A. **What is the main thrust of Jesus' answer when the disciples ask Him for the timetable of His second coming?** Mark 13:1-4 Mark 13:5 Mark 13:21-23

B. **Why should opposition and persecution increase our confidence that Christ will come again?** Mark 13: 9-10 Mark 13: 11-13 Luke 21:8-19

C. **With increasing tribulation, what comfort is it to *know* that Christ will return?** Mark 13:23 Mark 13:20 Mark 13:19

---

166.   Daniel 9 gives the background to this, especially verse 27. A detailed examination of that chapter is outside the scope of this book, and probably outside the ability of its author!
167.   Look at 1 Thessalonians 4:13-18.

Chapter 41
The second coming of the Lord Jesus Christ (Part B)

Disc **4** – Track **02**

Mark 13:24-37 (NKJV)
24 "But in those days, after that tribulation, the sun will be darkened, and the moon will not give its light; 25 "the stars of heaven will fall, and the powers in the heavens will be shaken. 26 "Then they will see the Son of Man coming in the clouds with great power and glory. 27 "And then He will send His angels, and gather together His elect from the four winds, from the farthest part of earth to the farthest part of heaven. 28 "Now learn this parable from the fig tree: When its branch has already become tender, and puts forth leaves, you know that summer is near. 29 "So you also, when you see these things happening, know that it is near—at the doors! 30 "Assuredly, I say to you, this generation will by no means pass away till all these things take place. 31 "Heaven and earth will pass away, but My words will by no means pass away. 32 "But of that day and hour no one knows, not even the angels in heaven, nor the Son, but only the Father. 33 "Take heed, watch and pray; for you do not know when the time is. 34 "It is like a man going to a far country, who left his house and gave authority to his servants, and to each his work, and commanded the doorkeeper to watch. 35 "Watch therefore, for you do not know when the master of the house is coming—in the evening, at midnight, at the crowing of the rooster, or in the morning—36 "lest, coming suddenly, he find you sleeping. 37 "And what I say to you, I say to all: Watch!"

Mark 13:24-27
It is certain!

After these alarming events and situations, Jesus describes the final 'curtain call' before He, *the Son of Man*, will return *in the clouds with great power and glory*.

Before He splendidly and majestically bursts on the scene expect unprecedented cosmic activity. *The sun will be darkened, and the moon will not give its light; the stars of heaven will fall, and the powers in the heavens will be shaken.* The coming to earth again of our mighty Lord, Saviour and Creator God, will be preceded by His angels gathering His chosen ones from far and wide. By God's grace, they have repented of their sins and trusted Jesus as their Saviour. God's prophecy is always future history. All this will certainly come to pass. We have Christ's own authority on which to base that confidence.

Mark 13:28–31
It is certain and it is near!

Jesus assures His hearers that *Heaven and earth will pass away, but My words will by no means pass away.* Thirteen times in Mark's Gospel,[168] underlining their importance, Jesus says, *Assuredly, I say to you.* Now He follows them with, *this generation will by no means pass away till all these things take place.* By *this generation,* He means that the generation of people first experiencing the final signs of His coming will still be there when He comes. He will come quickly. When the cauldron of fulfilled predictions really boils, His coming will follow speedily.

No one on earth knows when that will be. Futile attempts of some to predict it made them look very silly. As growth in the fig tree's leaves indicate summer's arrival, so these signs announce Christ's coming again. People need to come to Christ soon to escape being lost eternally. Jesus may come much earlier than they expect (if they expect Him at all). It is also essential that Christians live faithfully for Him. He may also come much sooner than some Christians think!

---

168. The following references are all from Mark's Gospel: 3:28; 6:11; 8:12; 9:1; 9:41; 10:15; 10:29; 11:23; 12:43; 13:30; 14:9; 14:18; 14:25; 14:30.

Mark 13:32-37
It is certain, it is near and it is challenging

Only God the Father knows the timetable. The angels know nothing. Even Jesus chooses not to know its timing in humbling Himself to take on our humanity so he can go to the cross to bear our sins in our place.

Someone has said that the Christian should live 'as if Jesus died this morning, rose this afternoon, ascended to Heaven this evening, and is coming back tonight.' Jesus warns, *Take heed, watch and pray; for you do not know when the time is.* We should live focused on that command. Anything diluting that is wrong. Jesus talks of servants and a doorkeeper. Their boss, the house owner, leaves, does no know or say when he will return and his servants know neither the day nor time of his return - dawn, morning, afternoon, evening, or during the night. So they must be ready for him. Jesus tells us all to be ready. He says, *Watch!*

Questions on Chapter 41
Mark 13:24-37 The second coming of the Lord Jesus Christ (Part B).

A. **Why can you be absolutely certain that Christ will come again?** Mark 13:31
John 14:3 2 Thessalonians 1:7-10

B. **As a fig tree's growth signals the coming summer, what will signal Christ's return?** Mark 13: 28-30 Mark 13: 24-27

C. **What is the main challenge to the Christian about Christ's second coming?** Mark 13:32-37 1 John 3:2-3 Matthew 25:1-13

Mark 14:1-11 (NKJV)
[1] After two days it was the Passover and the Feast of Unleavened Bread. And the chief priests and the scribes sought how they might take Him by trickery and put Him to death. [2] But they said, "Not during the feast, lest there be an uproar of the people." [3] And being in Bethany at the house of Simon the leper, as He sat at the table, a woman came having an alabaster flask of very costly oil of spikenard. Then she broke the flask and poured it on His head. [4] But there were some who were indignant among themselves, and said, "Why was this fragrant oil wasted? [5] "For it might have been sold for more than three hundred denarii and given to the poor." And they criticized her sharply. [6] But Jesus said, "Let her alone. Why do you trouble her? She has done a good work for Me. [7] "For you have the poor with you always, and whenever you wish you may do them good; but Me you do not have always. [8] "She has done what she could. She has come beforehand to anoint My body for burial. [9] "Assuredly, I say to you, wherever this gospel is preached in the whole world, what this woman has done will also be told as a memorial to her." [10] Then Judas Iscariot, one of the twelve, went to the chief priests to betray Him to them. [11] And when they heard it, they were glad, and promised to give him money. So he sought how he might conveniently betray Him.

Mark 14:1-2
The plot to kill Jesus

It is the time of Passover and the Feast of Unleavened Bread. At Passover, Jews remember their escape from Egyptian captivity and tyranny. As God moved to judge the Egyptians, He told His people to kill a lamb—the Passover lamb—and apply as protection its blood to the lintel of the door. Anyone sheltering in a protected house escaped God's judgement. Where blood was on the lintel, God's judgement passed over that house.[169] Passover pictures a guilty sinner escaping God's righteous judgement against his sin by sheltering under the blood of Jesus, the Lamb of God, by whose death on the cross he is saved. The Feast of Unleavened Bread recalls the Israelites' flight from Egypt to the promised land, with bread containing no yeast (or 'leaven'). In the Bible, yeast often speaks of sin's spreading influence. Anyone saved by Christ's blood must live a new life, by God's strength, marked by constantly turning from the 'yeast' of sin.[170]

Ironically, at this time of remembering God's deliverance, religious Jewish leaders plot to take Jesus by trickery to kill Him. In God's sovereignty their rebellion against Him will speed Christ's fulfilling the picture of the Passover Lamb of God. His blood will soon be shed to save sinners, captive to and oppressed by their sins. Trusting in His shed blood and receiving new life, they will cease to live under sin's dominion.

The chief priests and scribes decide not to take Jesus during the feast. That would cause a big uproar amongst the people.

Mark 14:2-9
Mary's costly flask of fragrant oil

Jesus eats in Bethany at Simon's house. Simon was probably formerly healed of leprosy by Jesus and is now back in society. A woman—identified in John's Gospel as Mary, Martha and Lazarus' sister[171]—breaks her flask of oil worth an average working man's yearly wages. She pours it over Jesus' head. Some criticise her *sharply* for wasting what could have been turned into cash for the poor. Judas is the disciples' (crooked) treasurer. Did he engineer criticism because an opportunity of dishonest gain disappears? Jesus defends Mary: the poor will always be there, but His time with them is now short. Mary's oil provides anointing of His body for burial in advance. Jesus' prediction, that Mary's generous loving respect for Him will be remembered worldwide, is true today. Mary now has her place in Scripture and challenges us to loving and generous sacrifice for Christ.

---

169. The account of Passover is in Exodus 12:1-30.
170. 1 Corinthians 5:6-8.
171. John 11:2.

Mark 14:10-11
The betrayer's wicked reaction

Is this the final straw for Judas Iscariot, who seeks prosperity by following Jesus (as treasurer![172]) He arranges to betray Jesus to the chief priests after the Feast. They gladly promise to pay him. He will soon betray the Prince of Life to death. How can someone so near to Christ for so long fail to trust and love the only One who can save him? Beware!

Questions on Chapter 42
Mark 14:1-11 Remembering—in advance!

A. How do the Passover and the Feast of Unleavened Bread picture the salvation from sin that Jesus Christ will bring? *Exodus 12:1-36 1 Corinthians 5:7-8*

B. Why is the woman (Mary) such a wonderful example and a challenge to us about how we should give to the Lord? *John 12:1-3 Mark 14:3-8 2 Samuel 24:21-24 Mark 12:41-44 2 Corinthians 8:9 Galatians 2:20*

C. Contrast Mary's attitude with that of Judas Iscariot. How are they each now remembered? *Mark 14:8, 10-11 Mark 14:9 Mark 14:11 Luke 22:48 Matthew 27:3-5*

---

172. John 13:29 tells us that Judas held the 'money box'.

Chapter 43
Passover

Disc Track
4 – 04

Mark 14:12-31 (NKJV)
12 Now on the first day of Unleavened Bread, when they killed the Passover lamb, His disciples said to Him, "Where do You want us to go and prepare, that You may eat the Passover?" 13 And He sent out two of His disciples and said to them, "Go into the city, and a man will meet you carrying a pitcher of water; follow him. 14 "Wherever he goes in, say to the master of the house, 'The Teacher says, "Where is the guest room in which I may eat the Passover with My disciples?"' 15 "Then he will show you a large upper room, furnished and prepared; there make ready for us." 16 So His disciples went out, and came into the city, and found it just as He had said to them; and they prepared the Passover. 17 In the evening He came with the twelve. 18 Now as they sat and ate, Jesus said, "Assuredly, I say to you, one of you who eats with Me will betray Me." 19 And they began to be sorrowful, and to say to Him one by one, "Is it I?" And another said, "Is it I?" 20 He answered and said to them, "It is one of the twelve, who dips with Me in the dish. 21 "The Son of Man indeed goes just as it is written of Him, but woe to that man by whom the Son of Man is betrayed! It would have been good for that man if he had never been born." 22 And as they were eating, Jesus took bread, blessed and broke it, and gave it to them and said, "Take, eat; this is My body." 23 Then He took the cup, and when He had given thanks He gave it to them, and they all drank from it. 24 And He said to them, "This is My blood of the new covenant, which is shed for many. 25 "Assuredly, I say to you, I will no longer drink of the fruit of the vine until that day when I drink it new in the kingdom of God." 26 And when they had sung a hymn, they went out to the Mount of Olives. 27 Then Jesus said to them, "All of you will be made to stumble because of Me this night, for it is written: 'I will strike the Shepherd, And the sheep will be scattered.' 28 "But after I have been raised, I will go before you to Galilee." 29 Peter said to Him, "Even if all are made to stumble, yet I will not be." 30 Jesus said to him, "Assuredly, I say to you that today, even this night, before the rooster crows twice, you will deny Me three times." 31 But he

spoke more vehemently, "If I have to die with You, I will not deny You!" And they all said likewise.

Mark 14:12–16
Passover prepared

Christ's disciples enquire where to prepare for eating the Passover meal together. Jesus sends out two with specific and secret instructions, presumably to avoid detection and hostile interest until His time to die. In the city they meet and follow a man carrying a pitcher of water—normally women's work—to a house owner. They ask where the guest room is for celebrating Passover. As Jesus predicts, the owner shows them a large, furnished and prepared upper room. This will be a special Passover with His disciples before Jesus, the Lamb of God, is slain.

Mark 14:17–21
Passover kept

At the Passover together that evening, Jesus tells them that His betrayer is among them. Only Jesus and Judas know his identity. Each disciple, humbly unsure of himself, asks Jesus *Is it I?* Jesus says someone eating with Him is the betrayer. He must go to die through the prophesied betrayal, but Jesus laments, *woe to that man by whom the Son of Man is betrayed! It would have been good for that man if he never had been born.* John's Gospel records that Judas soon leaves to arrange his Master's betrayal.[173]

Mark 14:22–26
The Lord's supper

As they eat the Jewish Passover, Jesus gives the bread and the cup new meaning for His followers. Anticipating His coming death on Calvary, He breaks the bread to picture His body, broken on the cross. Then He uses the cup of wine to picture His blood *shed for many*. He will not drink wine again until after His death, when He will

---

173. John 13:30.

142

drink it new in the kingdom of God. This predicts, after dying on the cross for our sins, His powerful bodily resurrection and ascension into Heaven! As the hour of the cross approaches, they sing a hymn together and leave for the Mount of Olives. The first Lord's Supper is over.

Christians observe it regularly to remember Christ's sinless body broken for them and His blood shed to forgive their sins. The Christian church will remember Him like this until He comes again in glory!

Mark 14:27-31
Beware of rash claims!

Jesus says He is the Shepherd who will be struck that night. They, His sheep, will stumble and be scattered. He promises to appear to them again after His resurrection. Peter immediately and rashly claims, *Even if all are made to stumble, yet I will not be.* Jesus tells Peter that he will deny Him three times before the rooster crows twice. Peter insists that this will not happen: he will not fail. All the other disciples follow Peter's rash claim. Later, they all fail.[174] Beware of making rash claims and promises, impossible to keep without God's grace and help, and a close, obedient trust in Him.

Questions on Chapter 43
Mark 14:12-31 Passover.

A. **In how many ways do these verses show again that Jesus is in control?**
Mark 14:13-16   Mark 14:18, 20-21, 25, 28, 30

B. **Contrast Peter's over-confidence with Jesus' knowing he would fail. How should humility and trusting God interact?** *Mark 14:29-31   John 18:27   Luke 22:31-34   1 Corinthians 10:12   2 Corinthians 12:10*

C. **Of what do the broken bread and the cup of wine remind us? How does this relate to the fact that Jesus will come again?** *Mark 14:22-24   1 Corinthians 11:24-25   Mark 14:25*

---

174. Mark 14:50 says *they all forsook Him and fled* in his hour of capture.

Chapter 44
Gethsemane

Mark 14:32-52

³² Then they came to a place which was named Gethsemane; and He said to His disciples, "Sit here while I pray." ³³ And He took Peter, James, and John with Him, and He began to be troubled and deeply distressed. ³⁴ Then He said to them, "My soul is exceedingly sorrowful, even to death. Stay here and watch." ³⁵ He went a little farther, and fell on the ground, and prayed that if it were possible, the hour might pass from Him. ³⁶ And He said, "Abba, Father, all things are possible for You. Take this cup away from Me; nevertheless, not what I will, but what You will." ³⁷ Then He came and found them sleeping, and said to Peter, "Simon, are you sleeping? Could you not watch one hour? ³⁸ "Watch and pray, lest you enter into temptation. The spirit indeed is willing, but the flesh is weak." ³⁹ Again He went away and prayed, and spoke the same words. ⁴⁰ And when He returned, He found them asleep again, for their eyes were heavy; and they did not know what to answer Him. ⁴¹ Then He came the third time and said to them, "Are you still sleeping and resting? It is enough! The hour has come; behold, the Son of Man is being betrayed into the hands of sinners. ⁴² "Rise, let us be going. See, My betrayer is at hand."

⁴³ And immediately, while He was still speaking, Judas, one of the twelve, with a great multitude with swords and clubs, came from the chief priests and the scribes and the elders. ⁴⁴ Now His betrayer had given them a signal, saying, "Whomever I kiss, He is the One; seize Him and lead Him away safely." ⁴⁵ As soon as He had come, immediately he went up to Him and said to Him, "Rabbi, Rabbi!" and kissed Him. ⁴⁶ Then they laid their hands on Him and took Him. ⁴⁷ And one of those who stood by drew his sword and struck the servant of the high priest, and cut off his ear. ⁴⁸ Then Jesus answered and said to them, "Have you come out, as against a robber, with swords and clubs to take Me? ⁴⁹ "I was daily with you in the temple teaching, and you did not seize Me. But the Scriptures must be fulfilled." ⁵⁰ Then they all forsook Him and fled. ⁵¹ Now a certain young man followed Him, having a linen cloth thrown

> **around his naked body. And the young men laid hold of him,** [52] **and he left the linen cloth and fled from them naked.**

Mark 14:32-42
Jesus prays as his disciples sleep

Jesus leads His disciples to the garden of Gethsemane, asking most of them to sit there while He goes to pray with Peter, James, and John. He is troubled and distressed, sharing that His soul is *exceedingly sorrowful, even to death*. Intensely aware of the horror of His impending separation from God the Father, He must carry our sins in His body on the cross and bear eternity's concentrated punishment for them in our place so we can be forgiven. He, the Eternal One in pure humanity, must soon face death itself for us.

Leaving Peter, James and John, He asks them to *Watch*, which obviously includes prayer. He goes further, alone. In His humanity—even though sinless, righteous and fully surrendered to the Father's will—He asks if it is possible to avoid what is coming. He knows His Father can do anything. But, even in asking for the removal of His cup of punishment and suffering, He adds *nevertheless, not what I will, but what You will*. Twice He returns to find the three disciples asleep. Twice He asks them to watch and pray, just for an hour. He understands their willing spirit but their weak flesh. How can they now answer Him—perhaps recalling their earlier rashly promised allegiance? Jesus returns the third time. But they still sleep. Jesus draws this sad episode to a close. Unsupported in prayer by those closest to Him, He leads them to meet His betrayer, Judas, and the hostile mob.

Christians often fail to pray earnestly or long enough. We would fail less if we corrected that. Yet He loves and understands us, knowing our failures. We are weak. We need to ask His help and strength to pray more meaningfully to Him each day.

Mark 14:43-52
Betrayed!

Jesus' enemies dare not take Him in daylight. They fear the crowd will attack them. But taking Him in the dark risks getting the wrong person. The New Testament records that Jesus escaped from previous attempts, once by simply walking through them! It was not then the right time for Him to die on the cross.[175] So Judas' evil task is to greet Jesus with the customary token kiss, thus identifying Him to the watching armed mob, wickedly motivated by the chief priests, scribes and elders. He salutes Jesus with *Rabbi! Rabbi!* He kisses Him, as planned. The mob now apprehends Jesus. He asks why they have come armed. He is no robber. They did not take Him earlier when He was daily with them in the temple. He stands firm however, and declares *But the Scriptures must be fulfilled*. He knows how and why He must die, though innocent.

All His disciples now flee—including one who earlier severed the ear of Malchus, the high priest's servant. (John's Gospel identifies that disciple predictably as Peter. Luke records that Jesus heals Malchus' ear immediately.[176]) In shame Mark admits fleeing away naked. His Master's captors grabbed him by the linen cloth he wore. He left it in their hands and fled. Jesus is betrayed and forsaken by those He has loved and taught. May we who trust Jesus now ask for grace not to follow their poor example?

Questions on Chapter 44
Mark 14:32–52 Gethsemane.

A. Why do you think that Jesus is exceedingly sorrowful, even to death? What kind of things do you think would be in His mind based on His words elsewhere in Mark's Gospel? *Mark 14:34 Mark 10:32-34 Luke 14:41-42*

B. Why are the disciples sleeping instead of praying? What should be your attitude about spending quality time in prayer? *Mark 13: 37-42 1 Thessalonians 5:17 Luke 18:1 Philippians 4:6 Isaiah 40:31*

C. Contrast the attitudes of Judas and Jesus. What part does the Bible play in the thinking of Jesus at this time? *Luke 14:43-46 Luke 14:48-49 Luke 14:49 Psalm 119:1-7*

---

175.   Read John 8:59, John 7:30; John 7:44 and compare them with John 18:6 when it is so obvious that Jesus clearly had the power to overcome those who arrested Him. He did not exercise that power because His time to die on the cross was beckoning.
176. John 18:10; Luke 22:51.

Mark 14:53-72 (NKJV)
53 And they led Jesus away to the high priest; and with him were assembled all the chief priests, the elders, and the scribes. 54 But Peter followed Him at a distance, right into the courtyard of the high priest. And he sat with the servants and warmed himself at the fire. 55 Now the chief priests and all the council sought testimony against Jesus to put Him to death, but found none. 56 For many bore false witness against Him, but their testimonies did not agree. 57 Then some rose up and bore false witness against Him, saying, 58 "We heard Him say, 'I will destroy this temple made with hands, and within three days I will build another made without hands.'" 59 But not even then did their testimony agree. 60 And the high priest stood up in the midst and asked Jesus, saying, "Do You answer nothing? What is it these men testify against You?" 61 But He kept silent and answered nothing. Again the high priest asked Him, saying to Him, "Are You the Christ, the Son of the Blessed?" 62 Jesus said, "I am. And you will see the Son of Man sitting at the right hand of the Power, and coming with the clouds of heaven." 63 Then the high priest tore his clothes and said, "What further need do we have of witnesses? 64 "You have heard the blasphemy! What do you think?" And they all condemned Him to be deserving of death. 65 Then some began to spit on Him, and to blindfold Him, and to beat Him, and to say to Him, "Prophesy!" And the officers struck Him with the palms of their hands.
66 Now as Peter was below in the courtyard, one of the servant girls of the high priest came. 67 And when she saw Peter warming himself she looked at him and said, "You also were with Jesus of Nazareth." 68 But he denied it, saying, "I neither know nor understand what you are saying." And he went out on the porch, and a rooster crowed. 69 And the servant girl saw him again, and began to say to those who stood by, "This is one of them." 70 But he denied it again. And a little later

those who stood by said to Peter again, "Surely you are one of them; for you are a Galilean, and your speech shows it." [71] Then he began to curse and swear, "I do not know this Man of whom you speak!" [72] A second time the rooster crowed. Then Peter called to mind the word that Jesus had said to him, "Before the rooster crows twice, you will deny Me three times." And when he thought about it, he wept.

Mark 14:53-65
Trumped up charges

Peter follows the arresting mob from afar as they lead Jesus to the high priest. He warms himself with the servants in the courtyard. Meanwhile, the first unlawful hearing takes place designed to find Jesus guilty. The death penalty must be exacted, though it is constitutionally impossible in Roman jurisdiction to hear Jewish charges! Again, the religious leaders lead the prejudiced injustice. The high priest and Sanhedrin (their council), seeking to kill Jesus, cannot establish any case even by their own perverted standards of justice. No two witnesses can be made to agree, and all are false. Even twisting Jesus' earlier figurative words, when He prophesied His resurrection, achieves nothing. Even their tailor-made, trumped-up evidence cannot be falsely corroborated!

So the high priest assumes the prosecutor's role, attacking Jesus for maintaining silence. Jesus refuses to answer the corrupt witnesses. However, when the high priest asks directly, *Are You the Christ, the Son of the Blessed?*, Jesus will not deny it. He says *I am* ('I AM' is an Old Testament name for God[177]) and confirms that He, the *Son of Man*, will come again *sitting at the right hand of Power, and coming with the clouds of Heaven*. Led by the high priest, they now find Him guilty of blasphemy: Jesus has claimed deity by His own words. They sentence Him to death, again completely unconstitutionally. Physical abuse follows. Jesus is spat upon, blindfolded, beaten, and ridiculed. Even the officers slap Him.

Consider this. Jesus is spotless, righteous and innocent. He suffers all this for sinners like you and me. His death on the cross in our place is for our sins.

177. Exodus 3:14.

Mark 14:66-72
Pathetic Peter

The high priest's servant girl recognises Peter, warming himself at the fireside of his Master's enemies. She identifies Peter, first to him and then to bystanders. Twice Peter denies it. The rooster crows after the first denial. Has Peter forgotten that Jesus said after three denials the rooster will crow a second time? He will soon hear the rooster crow again. Soon after his earlier denials he is challenged at the fire again, as some insist he is *one of them,* betrayed by his Galilean accent. Peter dishonestly rejects their allegations—now denying Christ for the third time—and starts *to curse and swear* and specifically mentioning Jesus in his wretched latest denial. He adds to his oaths, *I do not know this Man of whom you speak.* The rooster crows the second time. Pathetic Peter hears it, recalling the words of his denied Lord, *Before the rooster crows twice, you will deny Me three times.* He is broken. We read, *when he thought about it, he wept.* But are these tears of self-pitying remorse, or of deep hearted repentance for sin? The difference is huge. [178]We can confuse being sorry for ourselves with being sorry for our sins. Repentance requires sorrow for **sins**, not just for **self**! But for Peter, by God's amazing grace, true repentance—and a changed life—will follow later.

Questions on Chapter 45
Mark 14:53-72 When the rooster crows.

A. **What injustices against Jesus are there here? Did Jesus complain? Do you ever complain?** Mark 14:57-59, 62-64, 65

B. **What causes Peter to fall in the way that he does at this time?** Mark 14:54 Mark 14:66-71

C. **Why do you think Peter weeps? Contrast mere remorse with the Bible's teaching about real repentance and its effects.** Mark 14:72 Hebrews 12:17 2 Corinthians 7:10 2 Peter 3:9

---

178. Judas, for example, was full of remorse. He never repented. Remorse centres on a sinner being sorry for himself and the hurtful consequences of his wrongdoing . Repentance goes further. The sinner is sorry for his sin and turns from it to God. See Matthew 27:3 and compare it with 2 Corinthians 7:10.

Chapter 46
Confession and silence

> **Mark 15:1-5 (NKJV)**
> ¹ Immediately, in the morning, the chief priests held a consultation with the elders and scribes and the whole council; and they bound Jesus, led Him away, and delivered Him to Pilate. ² Then Pilate asked Him, "Are You the King of the Jews?" He answered and said to him, "It is as you say." ³ And the chief priests accused Him of many things, but He answered nothing. ⁴ Then Pilate asked Him again, saying, "Do You answer nothing? See how many things they testify against You!" ⁵ But Jesus still answered nothing, so that Pilate marvelled.

Mark 15:1
Unlawful imprisonment

The dishonest Jewish religious leaders keep Jesus in their custody. Thirsting for His blood, they consult in the morning with elders, scribes, and the full Sanhedrin. After unlawfully imprisoning Jesus, they compound their wickedness by binding Him and delivering Him to Pilate, the austere Roman governor of Judea between AD 26 and 36.

Mark 15:2
Unlawful question

Pilate's legal jurisdiction is Roman, not Jewish. Jewish religious issues, however important, are no concern of his or Rome's. Jesus nowhere disputes Rome's right to rule—He previously told people to give Caesar his dues.[179] Perhaps that is why Pilate,

179. Mark 12:17.

a man with a strict reputation, later finds no wrong in Jesus.[180] But now Pilate's question is irrelevant and unlawful in a Roman legal jurisdiction. He asks, *Are You the King of the Jews?* He knows that Jesus poses no political threat and his question has Jewish religious, not Roman legal, relevance.

Mark 15:2
Unhesitating answer

But as when responding to the high priest's earlier question, Jesus answers Pilate immediately in the affirmative, *It is as you say.* (There is no more emphatic Greek way of saying 'YES!') Jesus cannot, will not, and never does deny His character, office or deity. He is God, and a different sort of King. He always owns the truth about Himself. Today we need to hear that clearly. It is vital to know who Jesus is.

Mark 15:3-4
Unfair accusations

Again, Jesus will not answer the chief priests' false accusations. Pilate again asks why He refuses to answer their many charges. Sometimes, we too must ignore talk against us, but live so that we are known to be genuine. At other times it is right to put the record straight.

Mark 15:5
Unusual silence

Pilate marvels at Christ's silence, knowing that Jesus is truthful and honourable, unlike His accusers. If Pilate knew Jesus better, he would be even more staggered! Jesus is humbly silent before His wicked accusers, like a sheep being sheared. Yet simply, by His powerful word, He could despatch His opponents into a lost eternity. All power is His! Able to vindicate Himself completely, His wisdom is incomparable.

---

180. Luke 23:4.

Whenever challenged by opponents, Jesus shows total mastery in handling trick questions. Yet now the Innocent One remains silent. If He answers His accusers or punishes them, as He justifiably can, He will avoid dying on the cross as the spotless Lamb of God for our sins. His agenda is far nobler—an agenda of love, mercy, forgiveness, and eternal life for all who trust Him.

His silence is caused by innocence and impending sacrifice. Our silence often reflects guilt—we cannot think what to say. May God help us break our guilty silence to confess our sins to Him, and His amazing love to others.

Questions on Chapter 46
Mark 15:1-5 Confession and silence.

A. **What do you learn about Pilate?** Mark 15:1-5 Matthew 27:1, 11-25

B. **What kinds of questions does Jesus answer immediately and why?** Mark 15:2 Mark 15:3,5

C. **When is silence justified? Illustrate from Jesus' behaviour. How should that work out in your daily life?** Mark 15:3-5 James 1:19 James 3:2-13

Chapter 47
Anyone's son—Barabbas

Mark 15:6-15 (NKJV)
6 Now at the feast he was accustomed to releasing one prisoner to them, whomever they requested. **7** And there was one named Barabbas, who was chained with his fellow rebels; they had committed murder in the rebellion. **8** Then the multitude, crying aloud, began to ask him to do just as he had always done for them. **9** But Pilate answered them, saying, "Do you want me to release to you the King of the Jews?" **10** For he knew that the chief priests had handed Him over because of envy. **11** But the chief priests stirred up the crowd, so that he should rather release Barabbas to them. **12** Pilate answered and said to them again, "What then do you want me to do with Him whom you call the King of the Jews?" **13** So they cried out again, "Crucify Him!" **14** Then Pilate said to them, "Why, what evil has He done?" But they cried out all the more, "Crucify Him!"
15 So Pilate, wanting to gratify the crowd, released Barabbas to them; and he delivered Jesus, after he had scourged Him, to be crucified.

Mark 15:6–10
Background

Barabbas, a notorious prisoner, *is chained with his fellow rebels,* probably including the two criminals soon to be crucified on each side of Jesus' cross. Together *they had committed murder in the rebellion.* A strange and unjust custom obliges the Roman governor, here Pilate, to release at the Feast whichever prisoner the public request. Pilate's wants to release Jesus, whom he openly calls *the King of the Jews.* He knows that it is in envy that the chief priest wants Jesus killed. Pilate sees a potential ideal dual solution: deserved release for an innocent Man, and his own image enhanced, by pleasing the crowd. Will it work?

Contrast Barabbas with Jesus. Jesus never sinned. He always lived a righteous God-pleasing life, radiating holiness and loving compassion for everyone, even enemies.[181] Although a historical character, Barabbas pictures every human being. *Bar* means 'son of' and *abbas* means 'father'. He is the son, or child, of his father. So are we all! We are also the children of humanity's first father, Adam, and inherit his sinful nature. Because of God's grace, in sending His own spotless Son to die for us, we can become children of God by receiving Christ in our hearts. John 1:12 declares, *as many as received Him, to them He gave the right[182] to become children of God, to those who believe in His name.* Verse 13 teaches that they are not accepted because of their parents, or their own efforts, or some man-made religious plan. In receiving Christ by faith as their living Saviour they are born *of God.*[183] Having been *born again*, they receive God's forgiveness and a new nature.[184] They will never be the same again! Even a hardened sinner like Barabbas can become a child of God through turning from his sin and trusting Jesus personally to forgive him!

Mark 15:11–14
The wickedly wrong choice

The enormously influential rabble-rousing chief priests stir up the crowd to demand that Pilate frees Barabbas. Pilate, now reduced to pleading for Jesus, hears the orchestrated crowd's repeated and evil cry for Jesus' blood—*Crucify Him!* One hymn says 'a murderer they save, the Prince of Life they slay.' Jesus will die for sinners.

Mark 15:15
'I'd say it should be me there'

Pilate weakens under pressure. He releases Barabbas, scourges Jesus, and sends Him to be crucified, flanked by Barabbas' criminal friends. I showed an artist's impression of the crucifixion to a London prison congregation. The artist imagined recently released Barabbas, watching from the crowd as Jesus dies in his place. I

---

181. Hebrews 7:26.
182. The word 'right' is translated 'power' in the AV, and carries the sense of 'authority'.
183. John 1:12-13.
184. 2 Corinthians 5:17.

asked how my listeners would feel in Barabbas' place, seeing Jesus die flanked by his gang members. One inmate said quietly and respectfully, **'I'd say it should be me there.'**

He was right. When you know Jesus as your Saviour, you realise He bore your sins and punishment for them when He died for you on the cross. Would **you** now say, **'it should be me there'**? The real Christian is so grateful that Jesus is *the Son of God who loved me and gave Himself for me.*[185]

Questions on Chapter 47
Mark 15:6–15 Anyone's son–Barabbas.

A. Who is Barabbas? Why is he being set free? Mark 15:7 Mark 15:6, 8, 11, 15
Luke 18: 40

B. Who orchestrates the vicious opposition against Jesus? Does being a religious leader mean that the person concerned automatically knows God in his life? Mark 15:10-11 John 3:1-21

C. If after his release Barabbas did see Jesus dying between his two dying criminal friends, what thought would have struck him most? Do you see Jesus dying on the cross personally for you? Romans 7:24 Luke 18:13 Romans 5:8
Galatians 2:20

---

185. Galatians 2:20.

Chapter 48
At the cross (Part A)

Disc **4** - Track **09**

> **Mark 15:16-22 (NKJV)**
> [16] Then the soldiers led Him away into the hall called Praetorium, and they called together the whole garrison. [17] And they clothed Him with purple; and they twisted a crown of thorns, put it on His head, [18] and began to salute Him, "Hail, King of the Jews!" [19] Then they struck Him on the head with a reed and spat on Him; and bowing the knee, they worshiped Him. [20] And when they had mocked Him, they took the purple off Him, put His own clothes on Him, and led Him out to crucify Him. [21] Then they compelled a certain man, Simon a Cyrenian, the father of Alexander and Rufus, as he was coming out of the country and passing by, to bear His cross. [22] And they brought Him to the place Golgotha, which is translated, Place of a Skull.

Mark 15:16-22
Introduction

We will meet three times 'At the cross' in considering Mark chapter 15. Christ's cross and resurrection make biblical Christianity uniquely different from any religion. Religion teaches us to do something, join something, participate in some ceremony, or acquire some merit to lift ourselves to whoever or whatever God is considered to be. The message of Jesus' cross and resurrection is wonderfully different, emphasising that 'the way up is down.' Jesus, God the Son, came 'down to earth' in His incarnation. As the only perfectly righteous Man, He bore our sins and punishment so anyone trusting Him goes 'up to Heaven' after death. As God shows me my sin and guilt, I humble myself. In shame I confess my sins and guilt to God and ask for His pardon, freely available because Christ's blood was shed for me. As I go lower, Christ enters my life through His Holy Spirit and lifts me to a new level of living, even here on earth.[186] I receive eternal life and become what Jesus called *born again*.[187] Remember two important principles: 'the way up is down', and only Jesus Christ can save me from my sins.

Mark 15:16-18
Degradation

Now cowardly Roman soldiers cruelly abuse Jesus, whom Pilate called *the King of the Jews* and whom the Bible confirms is *King of kings, and Lord of lords*.[188] They lead Him into the Praetorium hall, the governor's official residence, and summon the garrison of about six hundred men. They dress Jesus like a king in purple. In a mock coronation, they crown His head with twisted thorns, taunting Him with empty insults, as king. Majorities and officialdom rarely honour Jesus, or those who follow Him! Today our King is still *despised and rejected by men, a Man of Sorrows and acquainted with grief.*[189]

Mark 15:19-20
Humiliation

Now they strike Jesus with a reed, spit on Him, and mockingly worship Him again, bowing their knees. (One day they will bow in terror at God's inevitable judgement.[190]) They humiliate Him, changing His clothes again. Jesus goes to be crucified. Our knees and heart should bow to Him in confession of sin and in willing surrender to Him as Lord of our lives.

---

186. A principle of biblical truth is that true humility before God attracts His blessing and uplifting. See 1 Peter 5:6.
187. John 3:3-7.
188. Revelation 19:16.
189. Isaiah 53:3.
190. Hebrews 9:27, Romans 1:18.

Mark 15:21-22
Compulsion

A sleepless night of cruel opposition leaves Jesus exhausted and weak from losing blood. Many victims avoided crucifixion by dying under that vicious Roman scourging. The soldiers randomly compel a stranger, Simon of Cyrene, to carry Christ's cross to Golgotha, a skull-like hill. No-one volunteers to help the One who has blessed so many. Simon is a North African with two named sons.

One son, Rufus, is mentioned in the book of Romans as a Christian.[191] Perhaps the soldiers' forcing Simon to carry Jesus' cross triggers events which lead people like Rufus to come to Christ? However, as already seen in Mark's Gospel, Jesus says, *Whoever desires to come after Me, let him **deny himself, and take up his cross**[192], and follow Me.*[193] To take up your cross means crucifying self to follow Jesus. It is a personal cross—the 'I' crossed out.[194] A real Christian takes up his or her cross daily to follow Jesus.

Questions on Chapter 48
Mark 15:16-22 At the cross (Part A).

A. Why does Jesus, the Son of Man, allow Himself to be bullied and beaten? Mark 15:16-20 Psalm 86:14 Psalm 140:4

B. When Jesus is mocked how does He react? How should you react if people mock you for being a Christian? Mark 15:19-20 Matthew 5:44

C. Consider Mark 8:34, Luke 19:17 and Mark 15:21. What does it mean to take up the cross? What ordeal must Jesus face as He takes up His cross? What does Jesus do for you in dying on His cross? Mark 8:34 John 19:1 Luke 9:2 Luke 14:27 1 Corinthians 15:31 Galatians 2:20 1 Peter 2:24

---

191. Romans 16:13.
192. My emphasis.
193. Mark 8:34.
194. This was so personal to the apostle Paul that he said, *I have been crucified with Christ; it is no longer I who live, but Christ lives in me; and the life which I now live in the flesh I live by faith in the Son of God, who loved me and gave Himself for me.* (Galatians 2:20).

Chapter 49
At the cross (Part B)

> **Mark 15:23-32 (NKJV)**
> **23 Then they gave Him wine mingled with myrrh to drink, but He did not take it. 24 And when they crucified Him, they divided His garments, casting lots for them to determine what every man should take. 25 Now it was the third hour, and they crucified Him. 26 And the inscription of His accusation was written above: THE KING OF THE JEWS. 27 With Him they also crucified two robbers, one on His right and the other on His left. 28 So the Scripture was fulfilled which says, "And He was numbered with the transgressors." 29 And those who passed by blasphemed Him, wagging their heads and saying, "Aha! You who destroy the temple and build it in three days, 30 "save Yourself, and come down from the cross!" 31 Likewise the chief priests also, mocking among themselves with the scribes, said, "He saved others; Himself He cannot save. 32 "Let the Christ, the King of Israel, descend now from the cross, that we may see and believe." Even those who were crucified with Him reviled Him.**

Mark 15:23, 25–26
Desolation

Jesus declines mixed wine and myrrh offered by the soldiers. Able to deaden pain, its main purpose is to drug the victim to stop him struggling while being nailed to the cross. Compassion is absent at Roman executions of murderous criminals. But Jesus needs no drug to stop Him struggling. He has chosen to go to the cross for us.

Those words *they crucified Him* are amongst the Bible's most poignant. Here at *the third hour*—nine o'clock in the morning—the universe's great Creator, bleeding and battered by His own creation, is splayed out and nailed to a criminal's cross. The title over Him, *THE KING OF THE JEWS*, identifies the rejected King who now bears our sins and carries our sorrows. Respect and compassion are missing—just *they crucified Him*.

Mark 15:24, 27–28
Realisation

A dying man nailed to a cross cannot influence ancient biblical prophecies about Him. But in the case of the eternal Son of God, they are being fulfilled as our sin-bearer hangs there bleeding.

Psalm 22 predicts the hands and feet of Jesus will be pierced, and adds, *They divide my garments among them, And for my clothing they cast lots.* As Jesus is stripped of His clothing, the soldiers unwittingly fulfil Scripture by dividing His garments amongst them and by casting lots for His clothing.[195]

Long before Roman crucifixion was invented, Isaiah prophesied[196] that, when dying, Jesus would be *numbered with the transgressors* as *He bore the sin of many.* Barabbas' two criminal accomplices are now crucified on each side of Jesus.

Luke's Gospel reports one of the two criminals abandoning his blasphemies and crying out to Jesus as he dies beside Him. The other one, sadly, does not.[197] Still, today, some in desperate need of forgiveness turn to Christ, while tragically others refuse to do so.

Mark 15:29–32
Temptation

The ignorant and vile mocking against Jesus continues unabated, gathering momentum. The chief priests' and scribes' example as Jewish leaders is vicious and cynical. They taunt a dying Jew, Jesus, with: *He saved others; Himself He cannot*

---

195. Mark 15:24
196. Isaiah 53:12
197. Luke 23:39-43

save. Let the Christ, the King of Israel, descend now from the cross, that we may see and believe. Would they like their loved ones to spend their last hours of life like that?

The by-passers follow their venomous example and join in blaspheming Jesus. Those refusing to turn from their sins to God easily parrot the objections and obscenities of others on the broad way to destruction. They repeat the dishonest 'spin' of Jesus' critics about destroying and rebuilding the temple in three days. They also mock Him with *come down from the cross.* As already noted, even the crucified criminals join in initially, as they speed towards a lost eternity which will make their present passing agonies seem light compared with the eternal punishment awaiting them. God graciously gives a late change of heart to one. He trusts the Lord Jesus as his Saviour, personally pleading *Lord, remember me.* [198]

The real 'Temptation of Christ' must be to *come down from the cross.* He possesses all the power, authority, and right to do so. Why does He stay nailed there?

'There was no other good enough to pay the price of sin.
He, only, could unlock the gate of Heaven to let us in.'

Questions on Chapter 49
Mark 15:23-32 At the cross (Part B).

A. **Consider the phrase 'they crucified Him'. Who are 'they'? How do you react to the Creator God bleeding and dying to become your Saviour?** Mark 15:24-26 Mark 15:1, 3, 8, 9, 11, 13-14, 15, 16, 22-23 Philippians 2:5-11 Acts 20:28

B. **What do the fulfilled prophecies of Psalm 22:18 and Isaiah 53:12 teach you about the divine inspiration and factual accuracy of the Bible?** Psalm 22:18 Isaiah 53:12 Acts 13:23-30

C. **If Jesus had saved himself by coming down from the cross, who else could He have saved from the punishment for their sins? By bearing our sins and judgement for those sins on the cross, who can He save now from eternal punishment?** Mark 15:29-32 Mark 10:45 1 Timothy 2:6 1 Peter 1:18-19 Isaiah 53:4-6 1 Peter 2:24

---

198. Luke 23:42.

Chapter 50
At the cross (Part C)

Mark 15:33-39 (NKJV)
33 Now when the sixth hour had come, there was darkness over the whole land until the ninth hour. 34 And at the ninth hour Jesus cried out with a loud voice, saying, "Eloi, Eloi, lama sabachthani?" which is translated, "My God, My God, why have You forsaken Me?" 35 Some of those who stood by, when they heard that, said, "Look, He is calling for Elijah!" 36 Then someone ran and filled a sponge full of sour wine, put it on a reed, and offered it to Him to drink, saying, "Let Him alone; let us see if Elijah will come to take Him down." 37 And Jesus cried out with a loud voice, and breathed His last. 38 Then the veil of the temple was torn in two from top to bottom.
39 So when the centurion, who stood opposite Him, saw that He cried out like this and breathed His last, he said, "Truly this Man was the Son of God!"

Mark 15:33-34

Separation

There was darkness over the whole land until the ninth hour. After three hours on the cross, from 9.00 a.m. until 12 noon, Jesus now suffers His last three hours in darkness, from the brightness of midday, until 3.00 p.m. (the Jewish 'ninth hour'.) That darkness veils from human view Christ's worst suffering—separation and punishment from His Father God as He bears our sins and judgement. His Aramaic cry, *Eloi, Eloi, lama sabachthani?* means, *My God, My God, why have You forsaken Me?* Just why is the incarnate God the Son now forsaken by His Father? The Bible answers, *Christ also suffered once for sins, the just for the unjust, that He might bring us to God.*[199]

---

199. 1 Peter 3:18.

One hymn says,

'Because the sinless Saviour died, my sinful soul is counted free.
For God the just is satisfied to look on Him and pardon me.'

Jesus, the eternal Son, is uniquely and once only separated from God the Father so
He can save us now and eternally from our sin and from God's wrath on it.

Mark 15:35-36
Misinterpretation

The use of *Eloi, Eloi*, causes some to think wrongly that Jesus calls for Elijah. They
misunderstand the meaning of Christ's death.

Many still misunderstand the cross today. Some think Jesus died only as an example
to follow. Others consider Him just a brave martyr, or an unhappy accident of history
the victim of man's cruelty. Often His physical sufferings are over-emphasised with
too much focus on His flogging and injuries. But the reason the spotless Saviour
died was to bear our sins and take the wrath of God's judgement for them in His
body on the cross. By raising Him from the dead, God the Father demonstrated His
acceptance of Christ's sacrifice for lost and condemned sinners. He will pardon any
who will come to Him on that basis.

Mark 15:37-38
Culmination

The four Gospels together contain Jesus' words from the cross.[200] Luke reports that,
before breathing *His last*, Jesus cries *with a loud voice* the words *Father, into Your
hands I commit My spirit.*[201] Jesus will not die until he has fully paid the punishment
for our sins. He then surrenders to death. Remember Jesus said, *No one takes* [my
life] *from Me, but I lay it down of Myself. I have power to lay it down, and I have*

---

200.   Luke 23:34, 23:43, John 19:26-27; Matthew 27:46, Mark 15:34, John 19:28, 19:30, Luke 23:41
201.   Luke 23:46.

power to take it again.[202] He now lays it down, to take it again soon through His resurrection. God now tears the temple veil from top to bottom, opening the way into the 'Most Holy Place'[203] through the death of His Son. The way is now open for any repentant sinner to come to Him!

Mark 15:39
Illumination

In the darkness, the duty Roman centurion is enlightened by God. He says, *Truly this Man was the Son of God!* and, as Luke records, he also says, *Certainly this was a righteous Man!*[204] He is right in both statements. Jesus, is our *Emmanuel*, or *God with us*,[205] dying as a totally righteous and completely spotless sacrifice for sinners, even for Roman centurions! Even for you and even for me! Do you know Him as your perfect Saviour God?

Questions on Chapter 50
Mark 15:33–39 At the cross (Part C).

A. **As Christ bears our sin, darkness falls over the land. Jesus, God the Son, is forsaken for the first and only occasion in time or eternity by God the Father. Why?** Mark 15: 33-34 1 Peter 2:24 1 Peter 3:18 Isaiah 53: 10-11 John 14:6

B. **What mistake is made about Jesus' cry on the cross? What mistakes do people make about the cross today?** Mark 15:35

C. **Consider how the Roman centurion responds at the cross to the death of Jesus. How does he also respond in Luke 23:47? Why do his two responses blend so well together?** Mark 15:39 Luke 23:47 Romans 13-4 Hebrews 7:26

---

202. John 10:18.
203. Mark 15:38.
204. Luke 23:47.
205. Matthew 1:23.

Chapter 51
He is risen!

Mark 15:40-16:8 (NKJV)
[40] There were also women looking on from afar, among whom were Mary Magdalene, Mary the mother of James the Less and of Joses, and Salome, [41] who also followed Him and ministered to Him when He was in Galilee, and many other women who came up with Him to Jerusalem.
[42] Now when evening had come, because it was the Preparation Day, that is, the day before the Sabbath,
[43] Joseph of Arimathea, a prominent council member, who was himself waiting for the kingdom of God, coming and taking courage, went in to Pilate and asked for the body of Jesus. [44] Pilate marveled that He was already dead; and summoning the centurion, he asked him if He had been dead for some time. [45] So when he found out from the centurion, he granted the body to Joseph.
[46] Then he bought fine linen, took Him down, and wrapped Him in the linen. And he laid Him in a tomb which had been hewn out of the rock, and rolled a stone against the door of the tomb. [47] And Mary Magdalene and Mary the mother of Joses observed where He was laid.

[Chapter 16]
[1] Now when the Sabbath was past, Mary Magdalene, Mary the mother of James, and Salome bought spices, that they might come and anoint Him. [2] Very early in the morning, on the first day of the week, they came to the tomb when the sun had risen. [3] And they said among themselves, "Who will roll away the stone from the door of the tomb for us?" [4] But when they looked up, they saw that the stone had been rolled away—for it was very large. [5] And entering the tomb, they saw a young man clothed in a long white robe sitting on the right side; and they were alarmed. [6] But he said to them, "Do not be alarmed. You seek Jesus of Nazareth, who was crucified. He is risen! He is not here. See the place where they laid Him.

7 But go, tell His disciples—and Peter—that He is going before you into Galilee; there you will see Him, as He said to you." **8** So they went out quickly and fled from the tomb, for they trembled and were amazed. And they said nothing to anyone, for they were afraid.

Mark 15:40-47
Important later evidence for the resurrection

Far from the crowd, *Mary Magdalene, Mary the mother of James the Less and of Joses, and Salome,* see Jesus die. They also observe where He is laid. Joseph of Arimathea, a Christian council member, on the day before the Sabbath courageously obtains Pilate's permission to take Jesus' body. He wraps it in linen, puts it in a tomb, and seals the tomb with a large heavy stone. Because Jesus dies sooner than Pilate expects, he first asks the centurion if Jesus is dead. He learns Jesus has been dead *for some time.* Pilate and the centurion are each accountable and dare make no mistake before releasing the body.

So the sealed tomb, now noted by the three women, holds Jesus' body, after certification of death. This forms valuable evidence supporting the historicity of Jesus' resurrection.

Mark 16: 1-8
No body!

Just after sunrise after the Sabbath—on the first day of the week or our 'Lord's Day'—the women come to the tomb to anoint Jesus' body. They worry about how to roll away the large heavy stone. Then they see it has already happened. Entering the tomb, they are shocked to see an angel—like *a young man clothed in a long white robe sitting on the right side.* He tells them not to be alarmed. He knows *they seek Jesus of Nazareth, who was crucified.* He proclaims, *He is risen! He is not here.* He invites them to *See the place where they laid Him* and sends them to tell Jesus' disciples—naming Peter specifically—that Jesus will go to Galilee. They will see Him there, as promised.

Some opposing Christ's resurrection claim the women were so sad, flustered and worried that they visited the wrong tomb and so could not find Jesus. But, having noted on Good Friday,[206] where the tomb's was, they know where to take the spices for anointing His body. Also, would all three of them make the same mistake about the tomb? 'Some argue that their being at the wrong tomb is supported by the angel's words, *He is not here.* But you cannot take only half of what the Bible says—take all or none of it for your authority. Having said *He is risen!* the angel immediately confirms, *He is not here.* The stone has been rolled away to let them in, not to let the risen Jesus out!

Mark 16:8
A natural reaction

Anyone fabricating this story would make the three women into heroes. But they act so naturally. *They went out quickly and fled from the tomb, for they trembled and were amazed. And they said nothing to anyone, for they were afraid.* Today we have rock solid evidence for the resurrection. But, first at the tomb, the three women are not in our position. Scared and confused, they keep quiet at first. Maybe people will think them crazy? Maybe they also think they are crazy!

But scared and confused people, like them, later become strong believers in Jesus and His resurrection! Doubting Thomas, the first recorded resurrection sceptic, also becomes a firmly convinced Christian![207] So does hostile Saul of Tarsus. Why?[208] Convinced by fact, they come to **know** that Jesus is alive! They meet the risen Saviour themselves. That makes all the difference! Objective evidence for the resurrection is supported by individual changed lives. You also can know the risen Lord in your life, if you trust Him as your Saviour who died for your sins in your place.

---

206. Mark 15:42; Mark 15:47.
207. Thomas moves from wavering scepticism to glorious certainty with the words, *My Lord and My God* (John 20:28) when He meets the risen Christ.
208. Read the testimony of this remarkable man who had his nature as well as his name changed (from Saul to Paul), in Acts 26:9-23.

Questions on Chapter 51
Mark 15:40 16:8 He is risen!

A. What facts here confirm the resurrection of the Lord Jesus Christ? Why is it important to demonstrate that Jesus really did rise from the dead? Mark 15:42-47 Mark 15:3-4 Mark 15:5-6 Mark 15:7 Acts 1:3

B. How do you know that the stone is rolled away from the tomb to let Jesus out, not to let people in? What biblical reasons can you give why Jesus' resurrection is absolutely vital? Mark 16:3, 6 1 Corinthians 15:12-19 Romans 1:1-4 Acts 2:32-36

C. Why do the fear of the frightened women, the unbelief of doubting Thomas, and the hostility of persecutor Saul (who became the apostle Paul) help to confirm that Jesus rose from the dead? What do their fear, unbelief and hostility turn into? Mark 16:8 Luke 24:9-11 John 10:24-25 John 20:26-29 Acts 26:1-2 Acts 26:1-23

Chapter 52
Resurrection, preaching, ascension

Mark 16:9-20 (NKJV)[209]

⁹ Now when He rose early on the first day of the week, He appeared first to Mary Magdalene, out of whom He had cast seven demons. ¹⁰ She went and told those who had been with Him, as they mourned and wept. ¹¹ And when they heard that He was alive and had been seen by her, they did not believe. ¹² After that, He appeared in another form to two of them as they walked and went into the country. ¹³ And they went and told it to the rest, but they did not believe them either.

¹⁴ Later He appeared to the eleven as they sat at the table; and He rebuked their unbelief and hardness of heart, because they did not believe those who had seen Him after He had risen. ¹⁵ And He said to them, "Go into all the world and preach the gospel to every creature. ¹⁶ He who believes and is baptized will be saved; but he who does not believe will be condemned. ¹⁷ And these signs will follow those who believe: In My name they will cast out demons; they will speak with new tongues; ¹⁸ "they will take up serpents; and if they drink anything deadly, it will by no means hurt them; they will lay hands on the sick, and they will recover."

¹⁹ So then, after the Lord had spoken to them, He was received up into heaven, and sat down at the right hand of God. ²⁰ And they went out and preached everywhere, the Lord working with them and confirming the word through the accompanying signs. Amen.

---

209. Many wonder why some translations of the Bible leave out Mark 16:9-20. Only in a very few early copies of Mark's Gospel (some say only two copies, one of which is flawed) are some or all of those verses missing. They are, however, found in the overwhelming majority of reliable Bible manuscripts. They are also cited from the earliest times by several early Church leaders. Those leaders' comments are said to predate those very few copies which do not carry those verses! Where did they get the verses from if they did not exist then? The author sees nothing in verses 9-20 to make him doubt their authenticity and so they are included here. Many have been blessed and challenged by these verses, which in any case are in no way inconsistent with the rest of Scripture and historically completely accurate.

Mark 16:9-14
Risen

Mary Magdalene, along with James' mother and Salome, is initially confused about Jesus' resurrection. Here we read that then she meets Him on the first day of the week and tells others who are mourning and weeping. They don't believe her. Then Jesus appears to two walking in the country. (They seem to be the two Emmaus Road disciples recorded in Luke's Gospel.)[210] Others also disbelieve them about the resurrection. Then Jesus meets the eleven disciples eating together. He rebukes their hard hearts for not believing those testifying about His resurrection. It is vital to come to know the risen Saviour and to share Him with others!

Mark 16:15-18
Preach

Jesus tells His disciples to preach the gospel worldwide to everyone.[211] Each Christian and church should join in doing that. Believers should be baptised. Personal belief in Jesus, His death on the cross for our sins, and His resurrection from the dead, precedes baptism. It is belief in Christ that saves, not baptism. Condemnation is for those failing to believe in the only One who can forgive their sins, not for those failing to be baptised. Specific signs will follow the gospel's advance into new areas, validating the Christians' message, work and service with the authority of the founding apostles. Those signs will mark them out as God's servants. Today our authority comes from a completed Bible—God's inerrant and infallible word.

Mark 16:19-20
Ascended

The risen Christ speaks to His disciples, ascends to Heaven, and sits at His rightful place on God's right hand. Our great and eternally living High Priest presents to Heaven His finished work of Calvary's cross for sinners! Meanwhile, His disciples go

---

210. Luke 24:13-35.
211. Mark 16:15.

and preach, with *accompanying signs.*

If you know Jesus as your personal risen and ascended Lord and Saviour, may you see the very best *accompanying signs* of people coming to trust Jesus through you! May they also see your different life and respond to Jesus Christ, as you explain how they can come to know Him by turning from sins and asking Him to forgive them, enter their lives, and lead them in His way! How glorifying this will be to God as you introduce them to *the gospel of Jesus Christ, the Son of God.*[212]

Questions on Chapter 52
Mark 16:9–20 Resurrection, preaching, ascension.

A. See verses 13 and 14. Does everyone immediately believe in Jesus' resurrection? How does risen Jesus talk to some of them? What does that show about the resurrection and God's ability to change people? *Mark 16:13-14 Luke 24: 13-35 Luke 24:36-49 1 Corinthians 15:3-9*

B. What are the main points of the gospel to be preached? Why should Christians share it with as many people as possible? *Mark 16:15 1 Corinthians 15:3-4 Luke 24:47 Mark 16:15 Matthew 28:18-20*

C. Could Jesus to ascend into Heaven, where He is seated now, without first rising from death? How is Jesus, as 'Emmanuel' ('God with us'), unlike any religious teacher, past or present? *Mark 16:9, 19 Acts 1:3, 9-11 Hebrews 10:12 John 19:30 1 Timothy 3:16 Ephesians 1:20 Philippians 2:9-11 Acts 4:12 John 14:6 Matthew 1:23*

---

212. Mark1:1—We finish Mark's Gospel where we started with *Jesus Christ, the Son of God!* How appropriate for the only One who is 'the same yesterday, and today, and forever'!

A Final Word

We hope you have been blessed and helped through the *Mark Time* book and CDs, and that you will recommend them to others. Why not join a *Mark Time* Discussion Course, or go through the *Mark Time* correspondence Course? Why not encourage others to do the same?

If you want to establish a regular daily quiet time with God, of reading the Bible and praying to Him, we hope *Mark Time* will help you. Start by recapping on Mark's Gospel. Later, why not go through the whole New Testament progressively, and follow that with the Old Testament and New Testament together?

Day One Publications' biggest book, *The Bible Panorama*, would help you tremendously. It walks you through the whole Bible, giving a brief overview of each book in the Bible before covering all the verses in each chapter of each book in sensible clusters very simply and easily to follow. Part 2 explains what the Bible is, how it can be studied, why it can be trusted completely, why the so-called contradictions are not really contradictions at all, how to get the most out of the Bible, how the contents of the Bible were decided, what is the Bible's central message, and why we should read it right through. It contains useful schemes to help you read through the Bible, either in a year, or at your own pace (quicker or slower!) *The Bible Panorama* comes with a free CD ROM so you can put its text on your computer.

If *Mark Time* has helped you to trust Jesus Christ as your Saviour, or encouraged your Christian life, please let us know. If that is so, seek out an established Christian friend and a Bible-believing church or fellowship which can support you spiritually. If you need further help or guidance please feel free to write to the publishers. at the address given in this book, requesting help and advice.

Nothing is more important in life than to come to know and follow the Lord Jesus Christ, who is the central message of the Bible and God's living Word, and to come to know and follow the Bible, which is God's written word.

Mark Time—The Book
& 4 Audio CD Set

Mark Time—Discussion Course

Mark Time—Correspondence Course

Try these *Mark Time* resources, which, when used alongside this *Mark Time* Book and audio 4 CD set, will deepen your enjoyment and knowledge of Mark's Gospel: the *Mark Time* Discussion Course—a straightforward way of stimulating discussion on Mark's Gospel with others; the *Mark Time* Correspondence Course—an enjoyable and simple method of getting the most out of Mark's Gospel and the *Mark Time* Book and CDs. Diplomas are made available for those who complete the course.

Good quantity discounts on all *Mark Time* resources are available on request to churches and groups who wish to run the *Mark Time* Discussion Course or promote the *Mark Time* Correspondence Course.

Also by Gerard Chrispin:

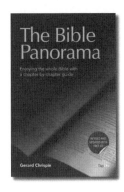

The Bible Panorama

The Bible Panorama is a unique introduction to and survey of the Bible, giving an overview of each book of the Bible and taking into consideration the message of each verse, without actually being a verse-by-verse commentary. It provides a series of very memorable outlines for each chapter of the Bible. It also includes a succinct but vigorous defence of the Bible, and concludes with a number of reading schemes to guide the reader through the Scriptures.

Day One Publications
Ryelands Road, Leominster, HR6 8NZ
tel—01568 613 740 fax—01568 611 43
email—sales@dayone.co.uk
web site—www.dayone.co.uk
North American—email—sales@dayonebookstore.com
North American—web site—www.dayonebookstore.com